Hearts in Abundance

photos by
Kim Timmerman

Copyright © 2021 Kim Timmermam
All cover art copyright © Kim Timmerman
All Rights Reserved

The photos in this book were taken by and belong to the author. No part of this book may be reproduced or transmitted in any form or by any means, electronic or mechanical, including photocopying, recording, or by any information storage and retrieval system, without permission in writing from the author.

Publishing Coordinator – Sharon Kizziah-Holmes

Paperback-Press
an imprint of A & S Publishing
A & S Holmes, Inc.

ISBN -13: 978-1-951772-59-8

DEDICATION

To my love Will. Without your true, genuine love this book would not be possible. Thank you for the suggestion, your willingness to help and your dedication in supporting me every step of the way. "Where there is a WILL there is a way."

I would also like to thank my son Tyler for always believing in me. He has supported all of my ideas no matter how outlandish they may be. Not to mention the patience he has of having to stop what we are doing along the way to capture the hearts as they present themselves.

I Love You Both with all of my ♡♡.

ACKNOWLEDGMENTS

For everyone in my life who has lifted me up, encouraged me to chase my dreams and never give up; thank you for believing in, supporting, and loving me through this journey.

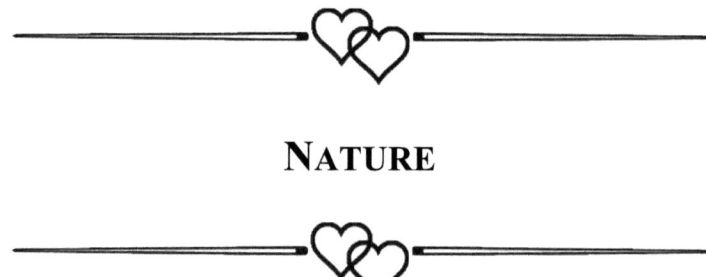

NATURE

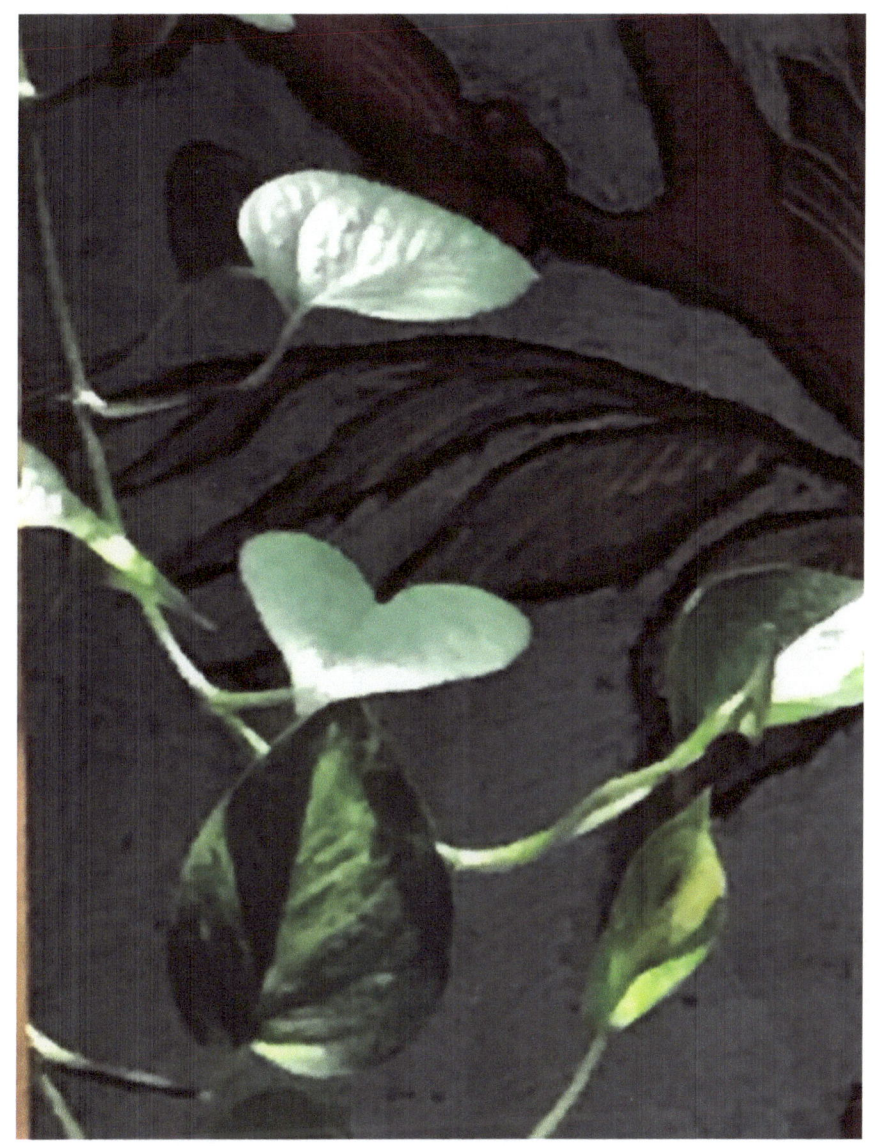

Restaurant Plant

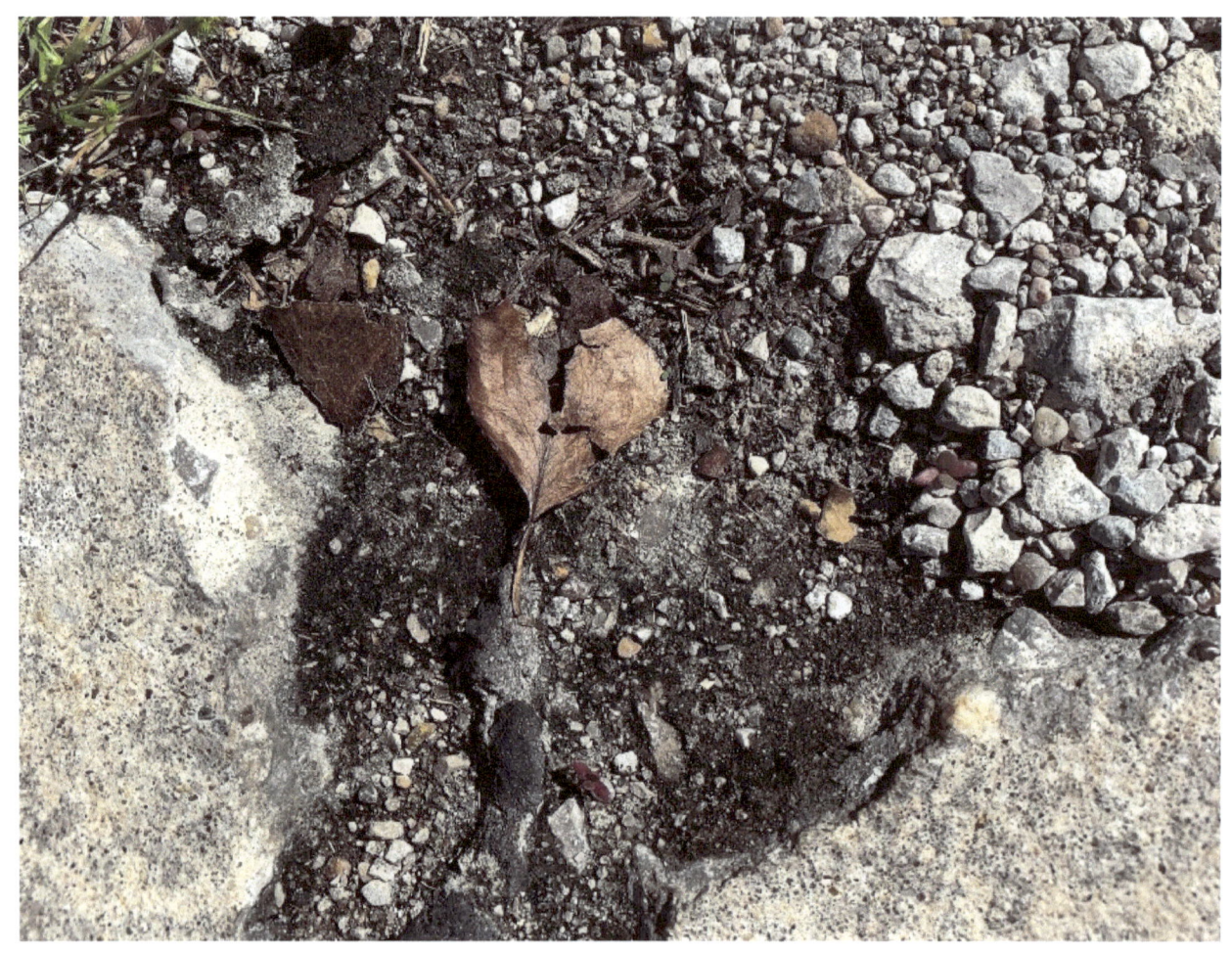

AT THE RIVER

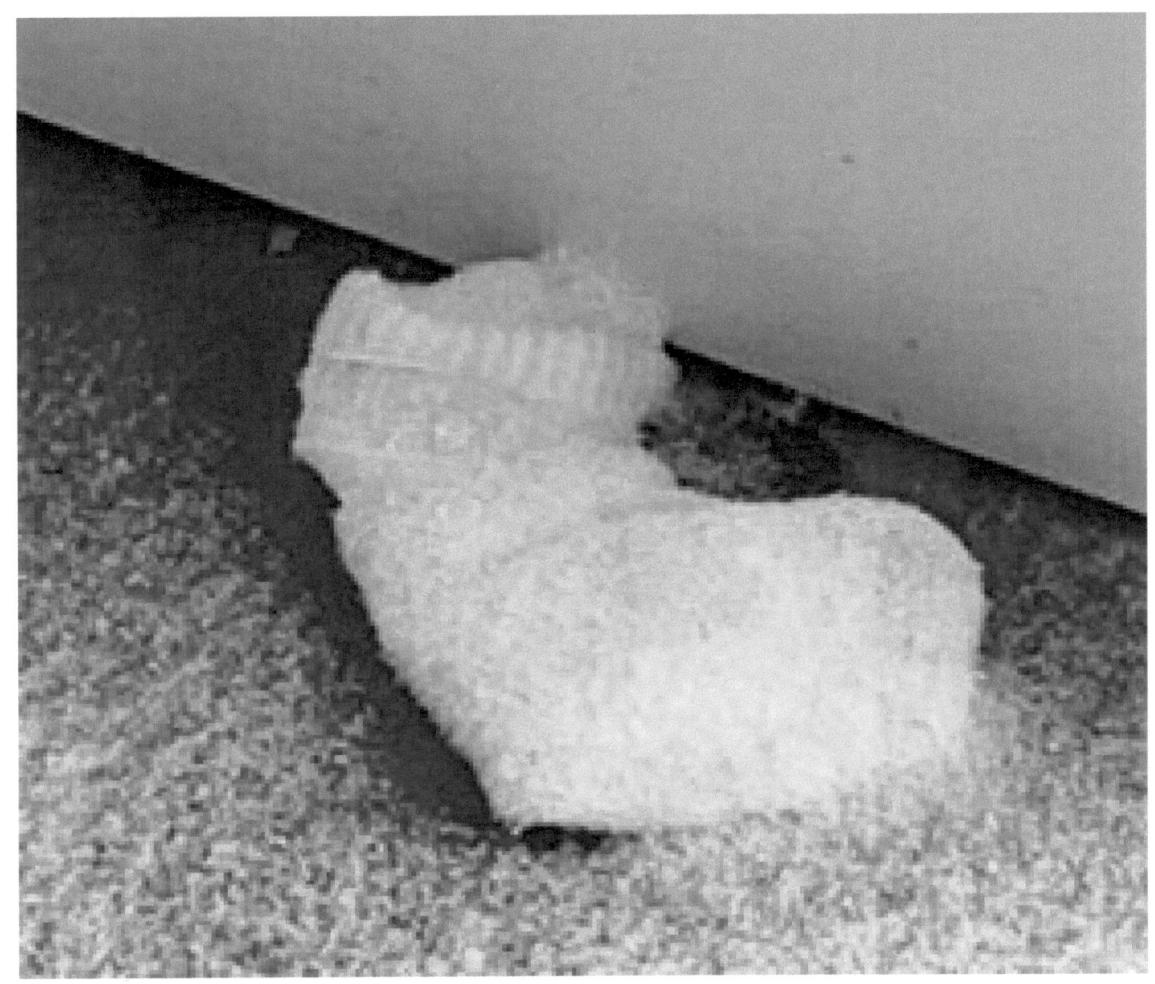

FRONT PORCH ICE

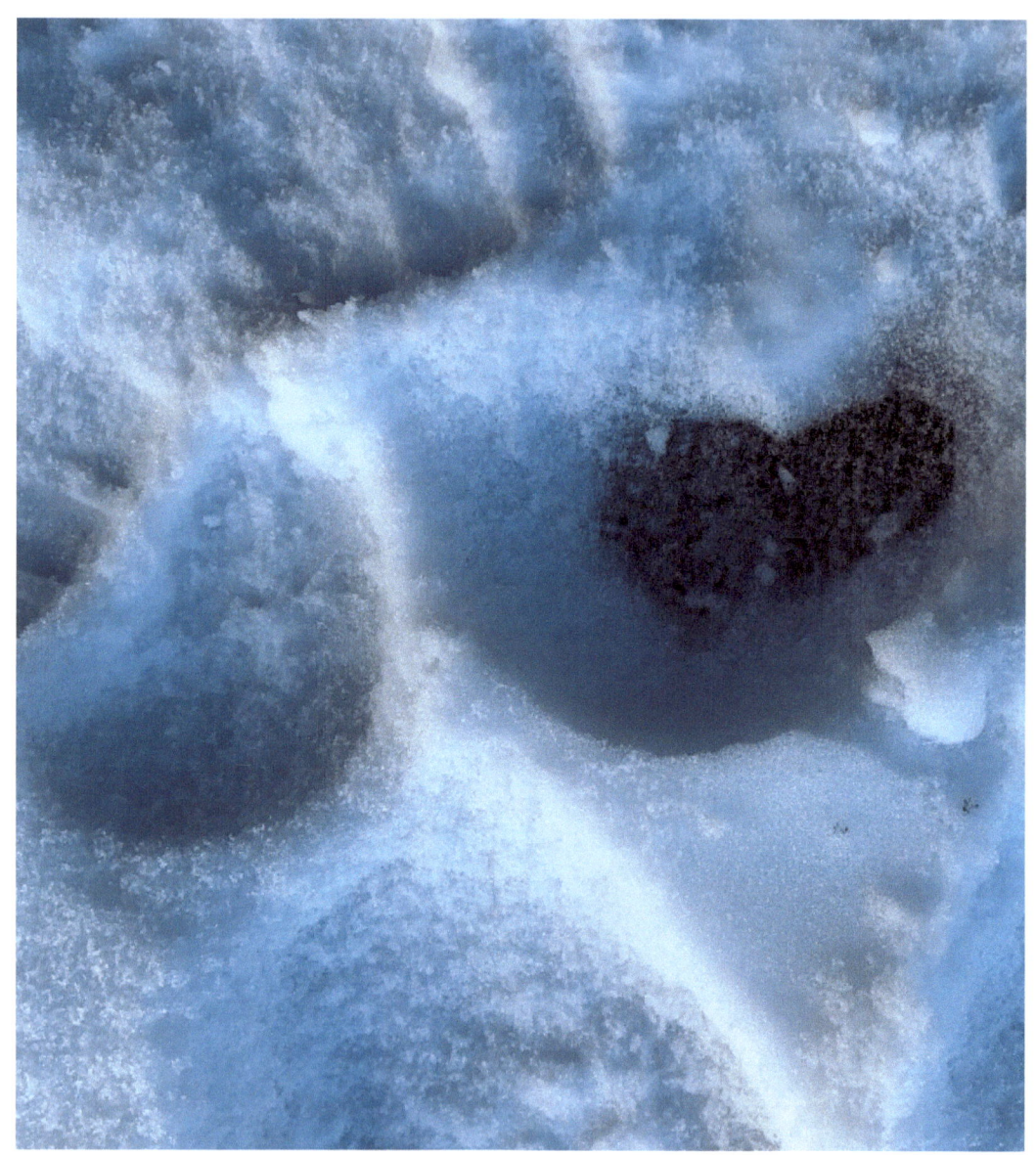

I SEE TWO. DO YOU?

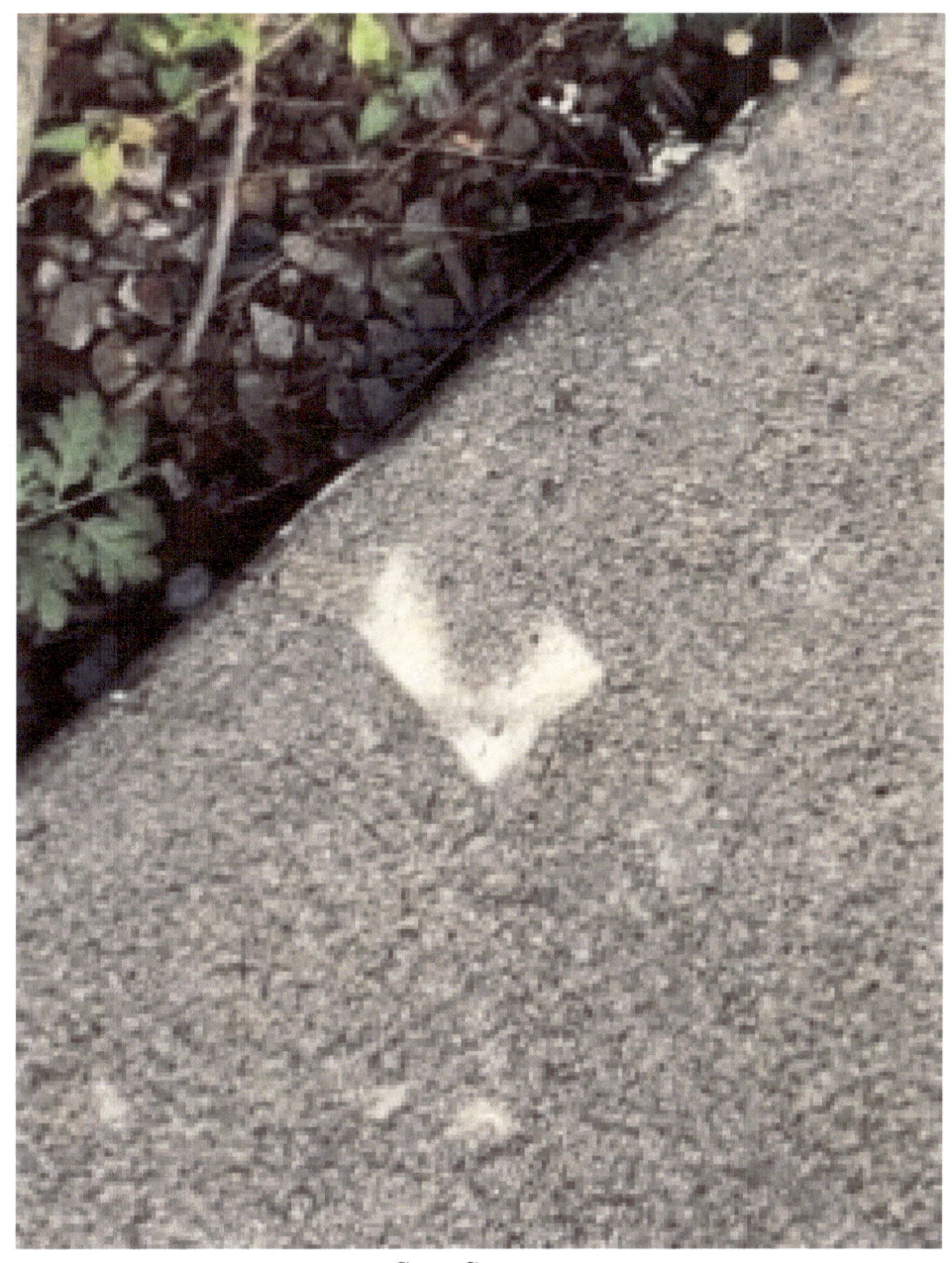

SUN SHADOW

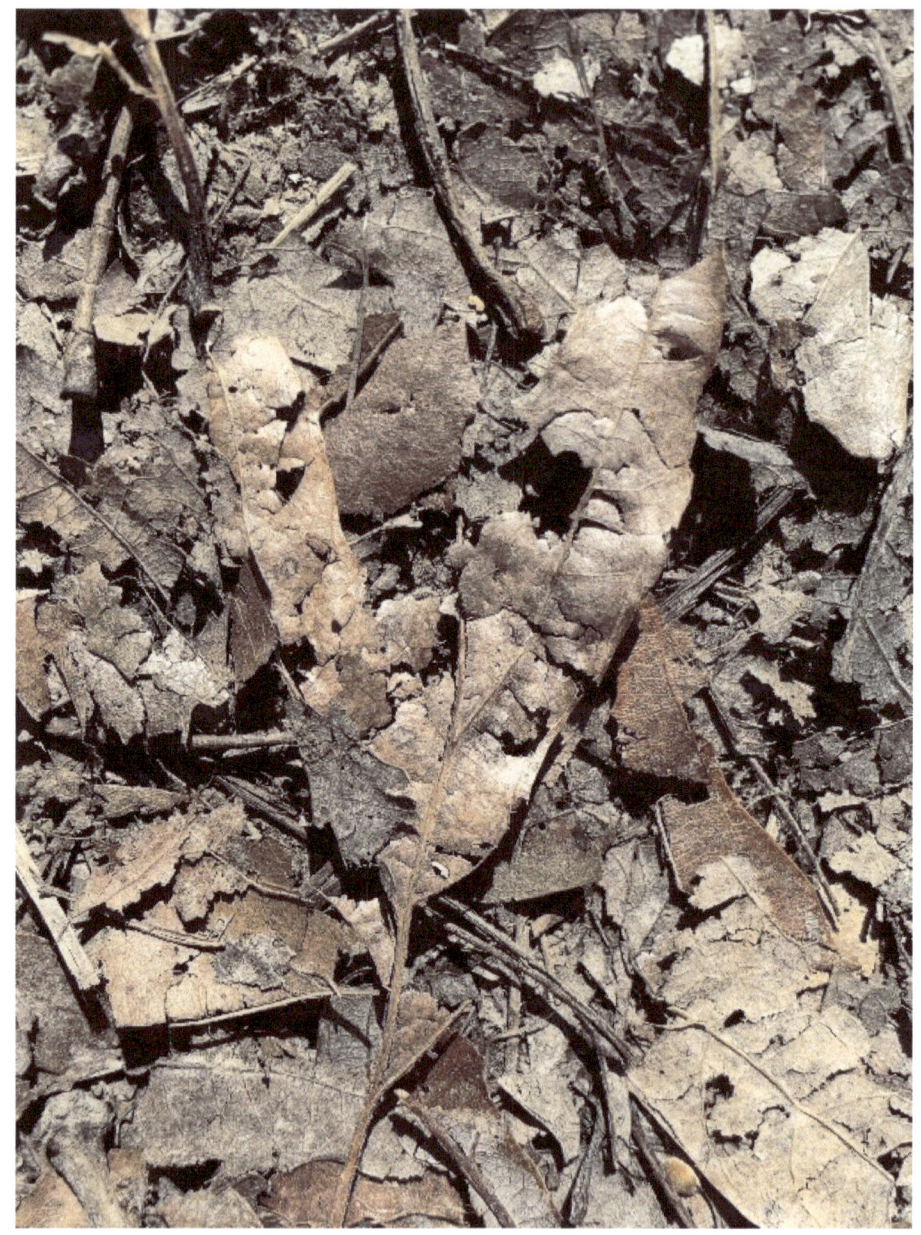

Leaf

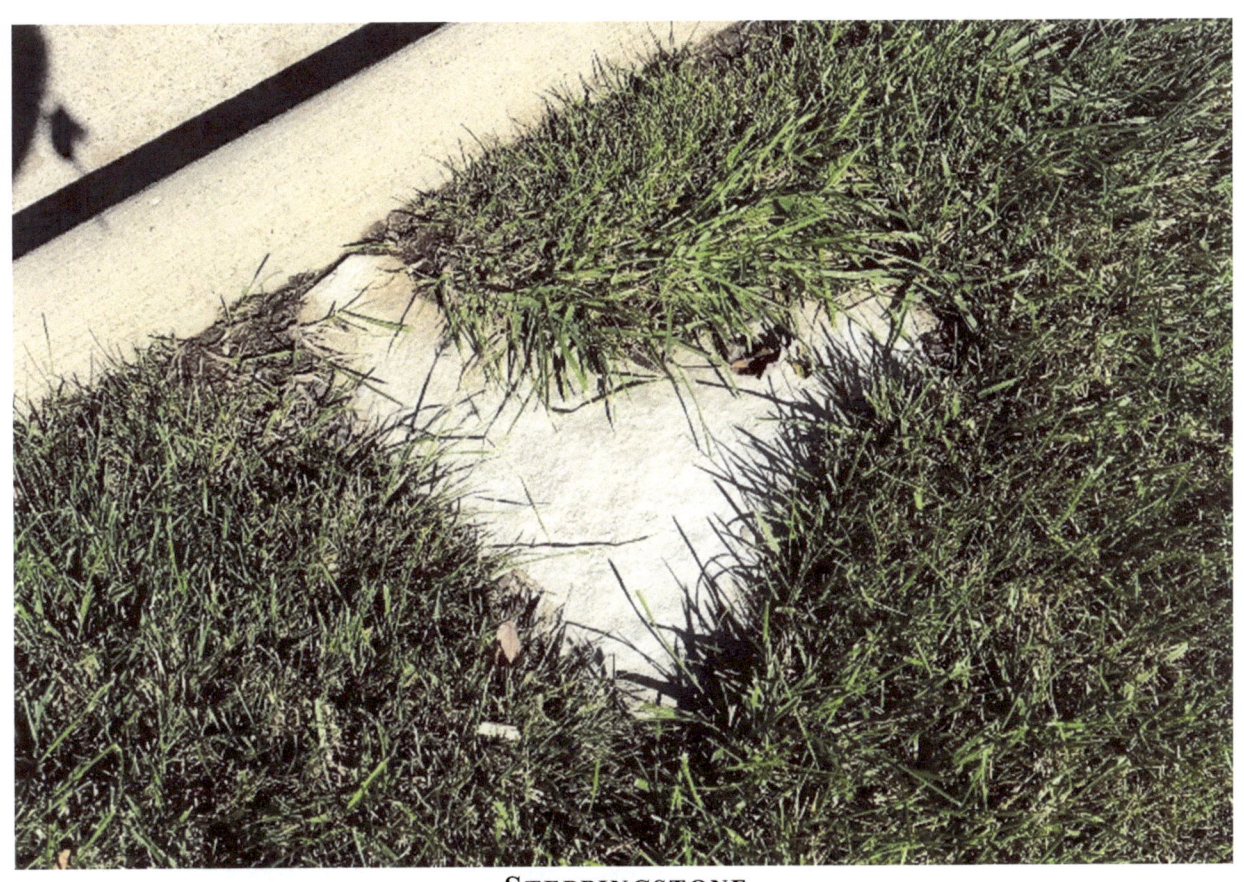
STEPPINGSTONE

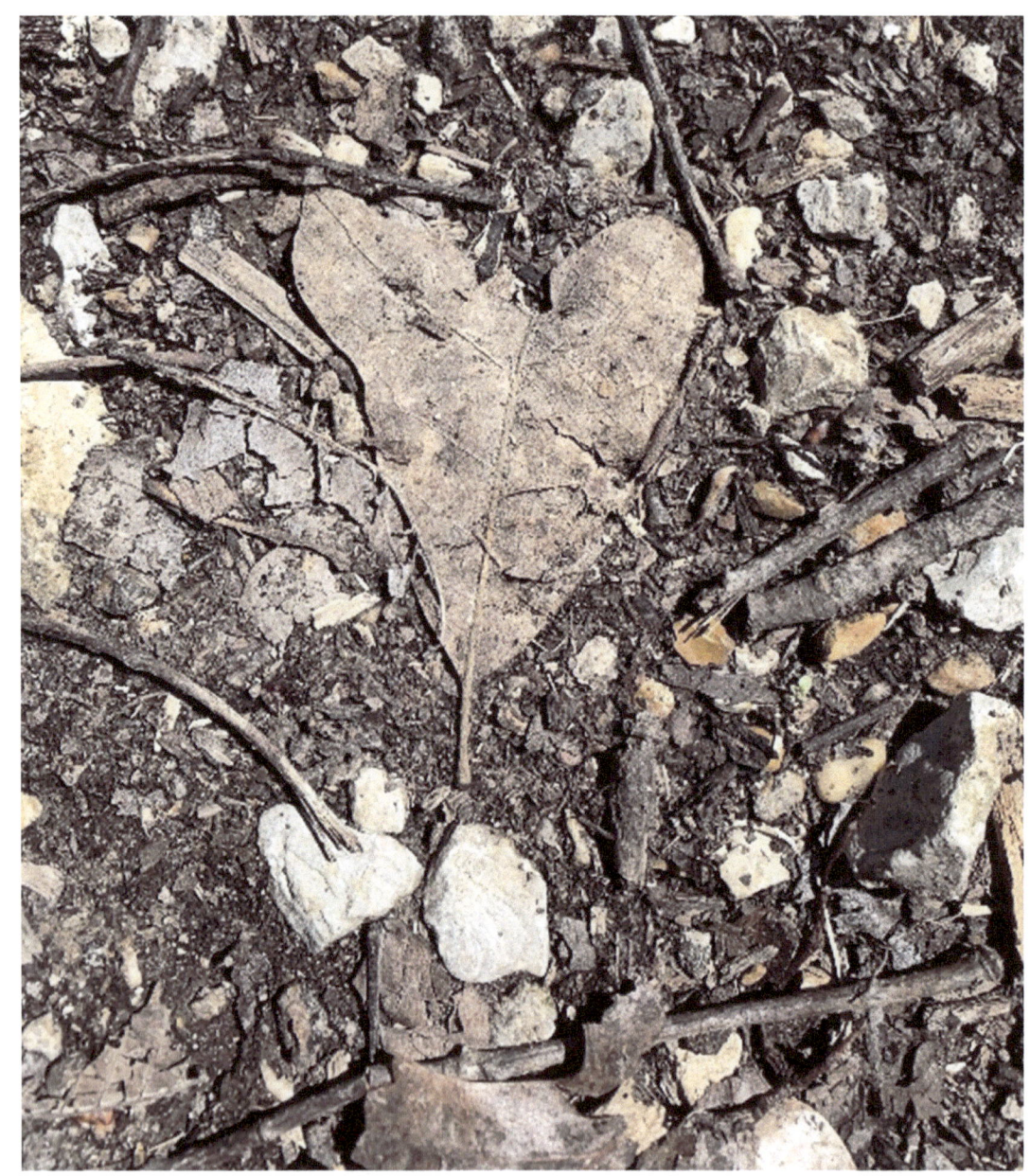

A Leaf & A Rock

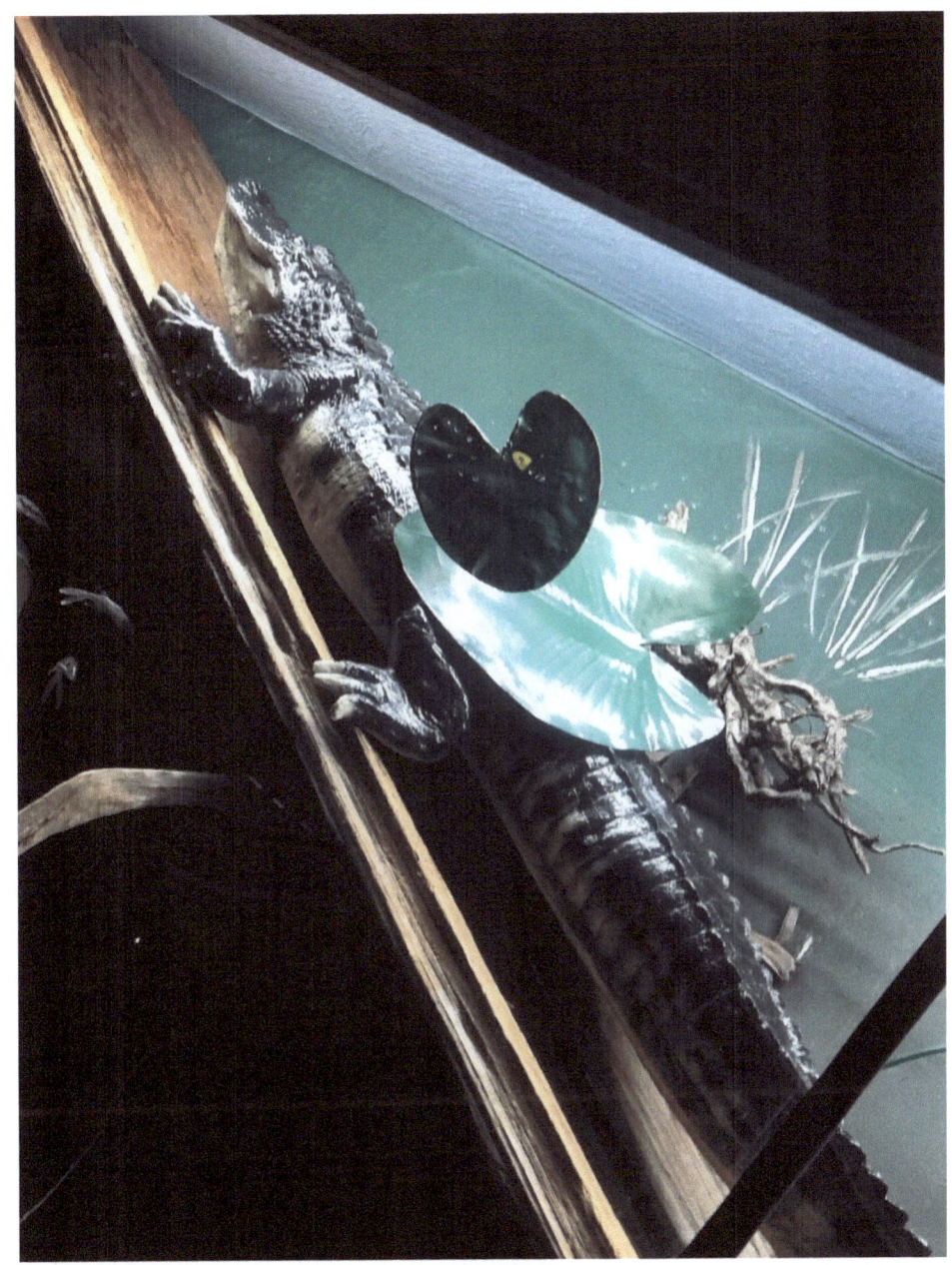
ALLIGATOR AQUARIUM

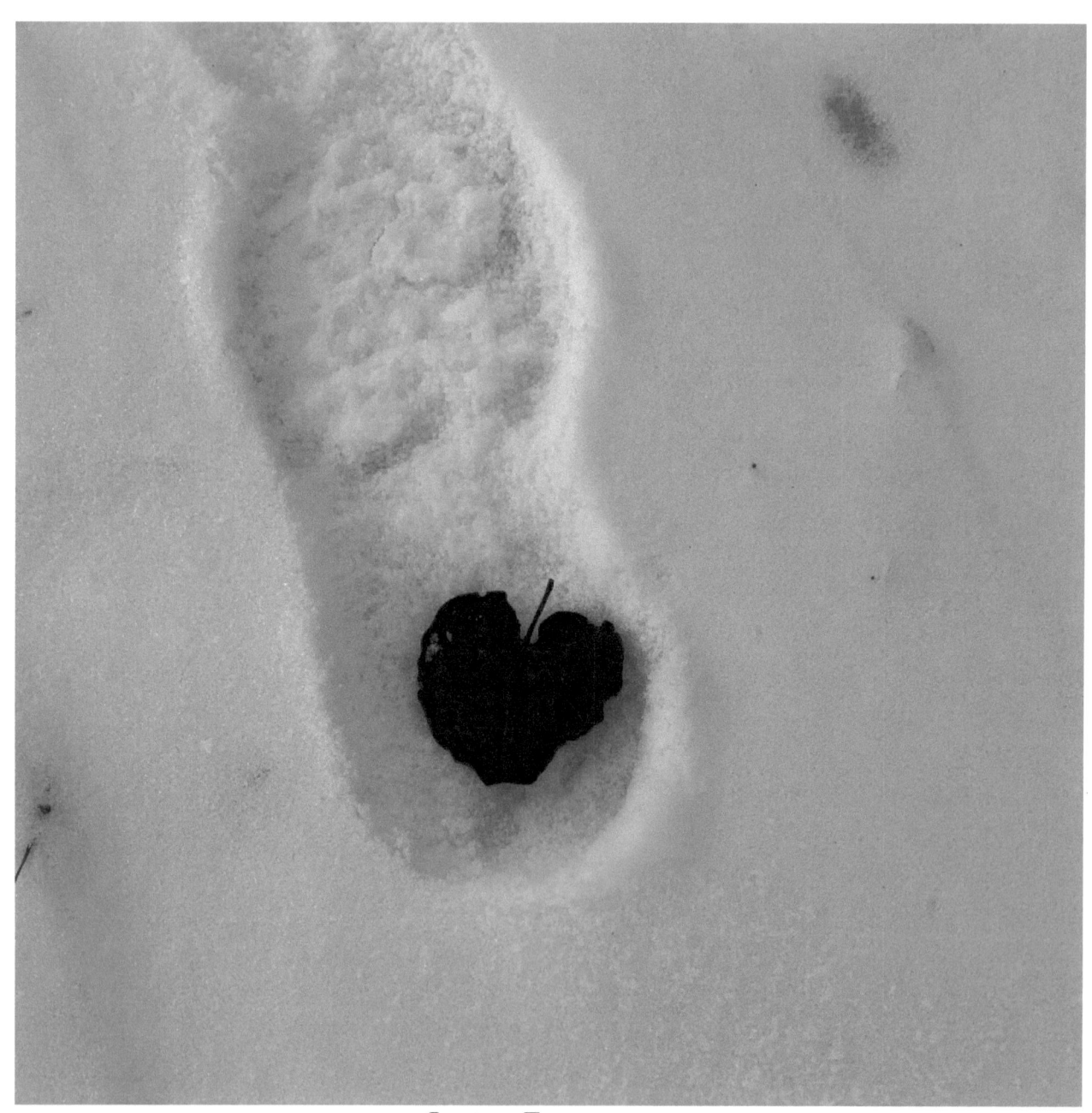

IN THE FOOTPRINT

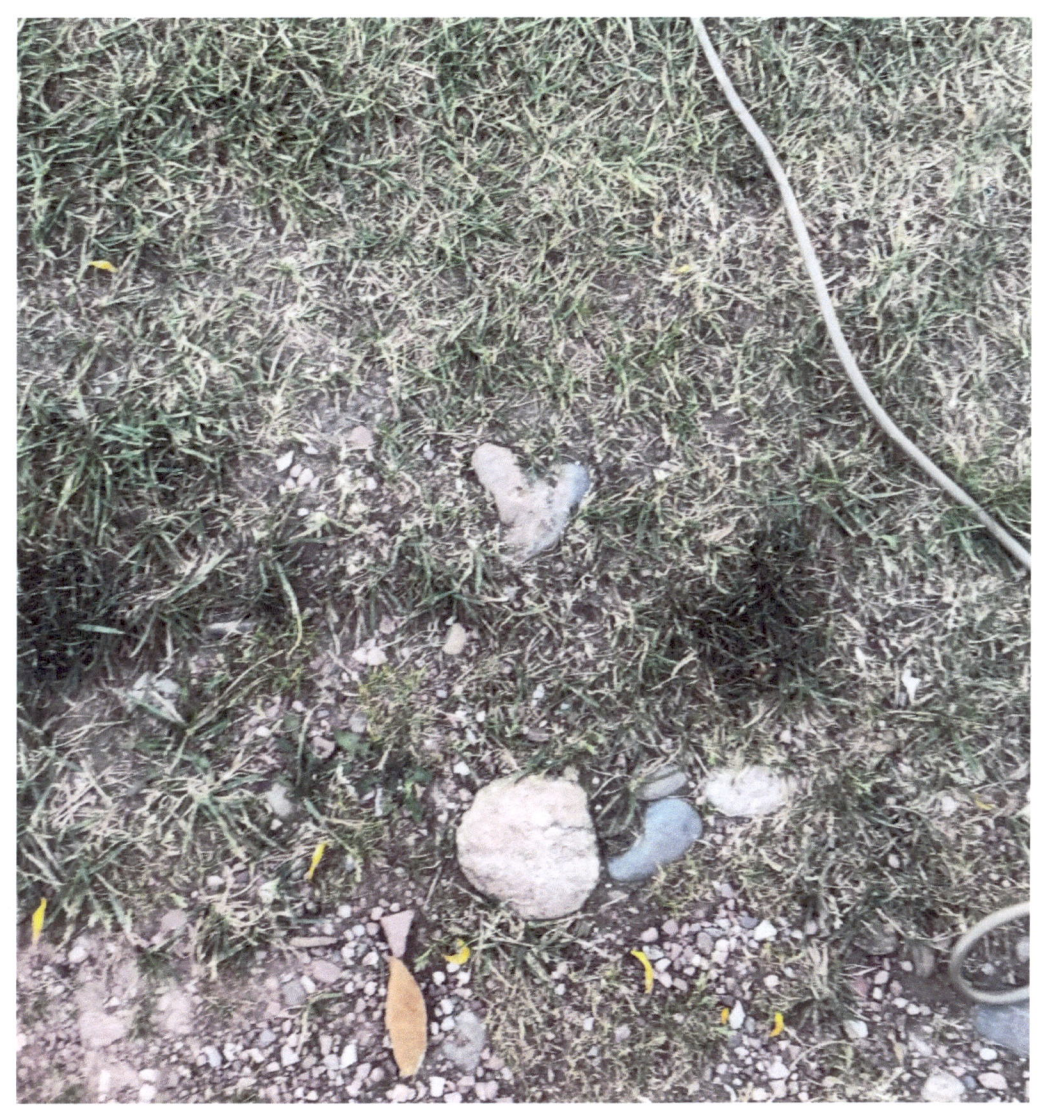

MUSIC FESTIVAL ROCK

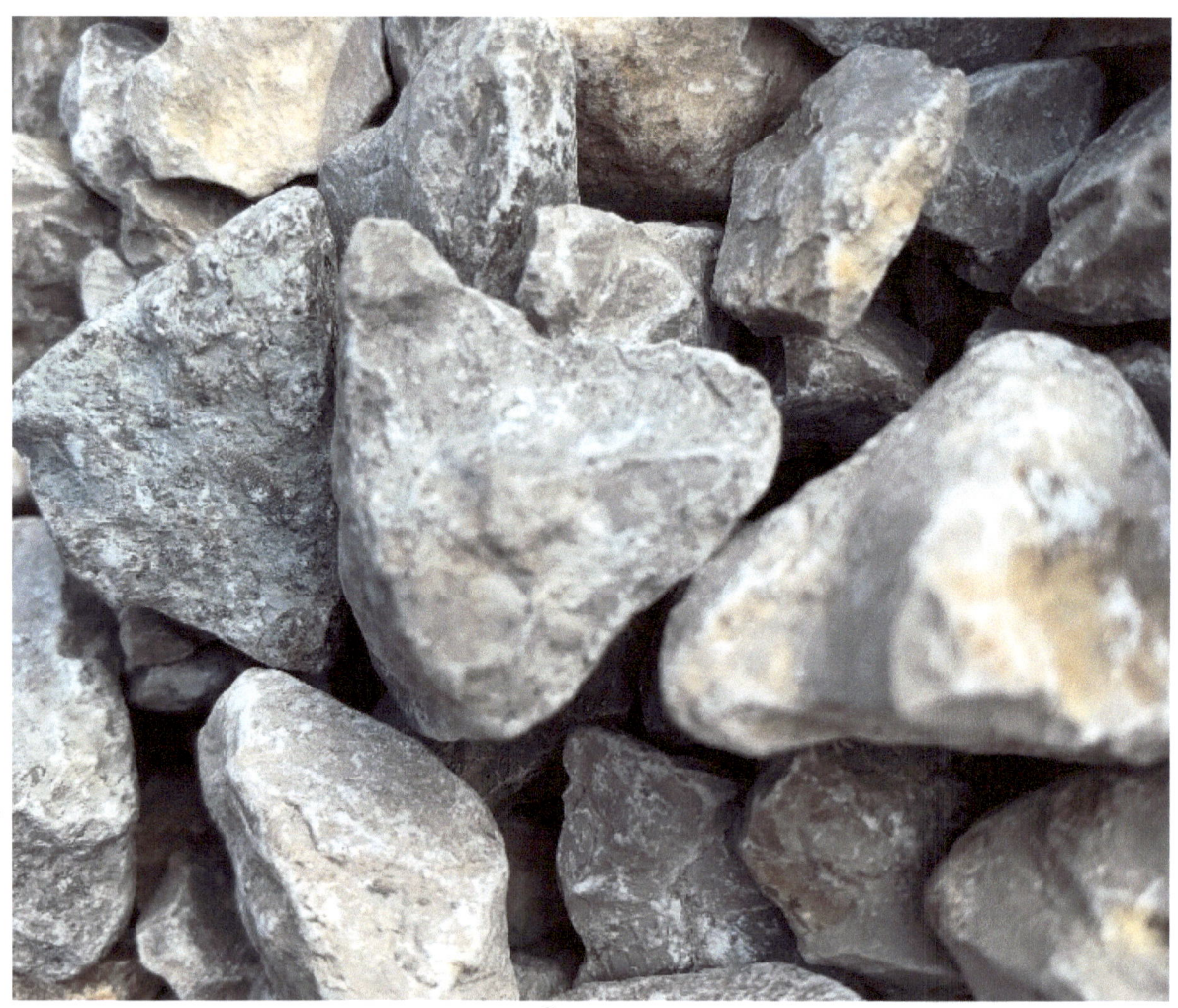

STONE

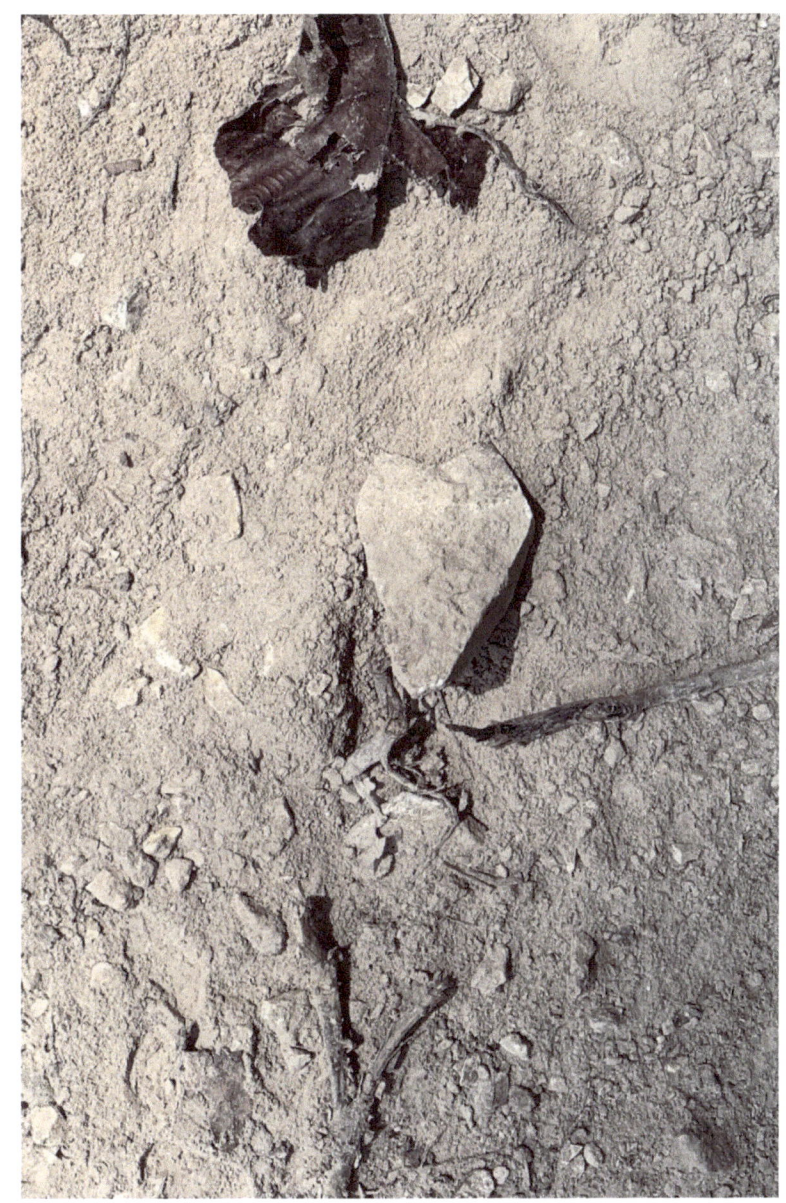

Dirt Rock

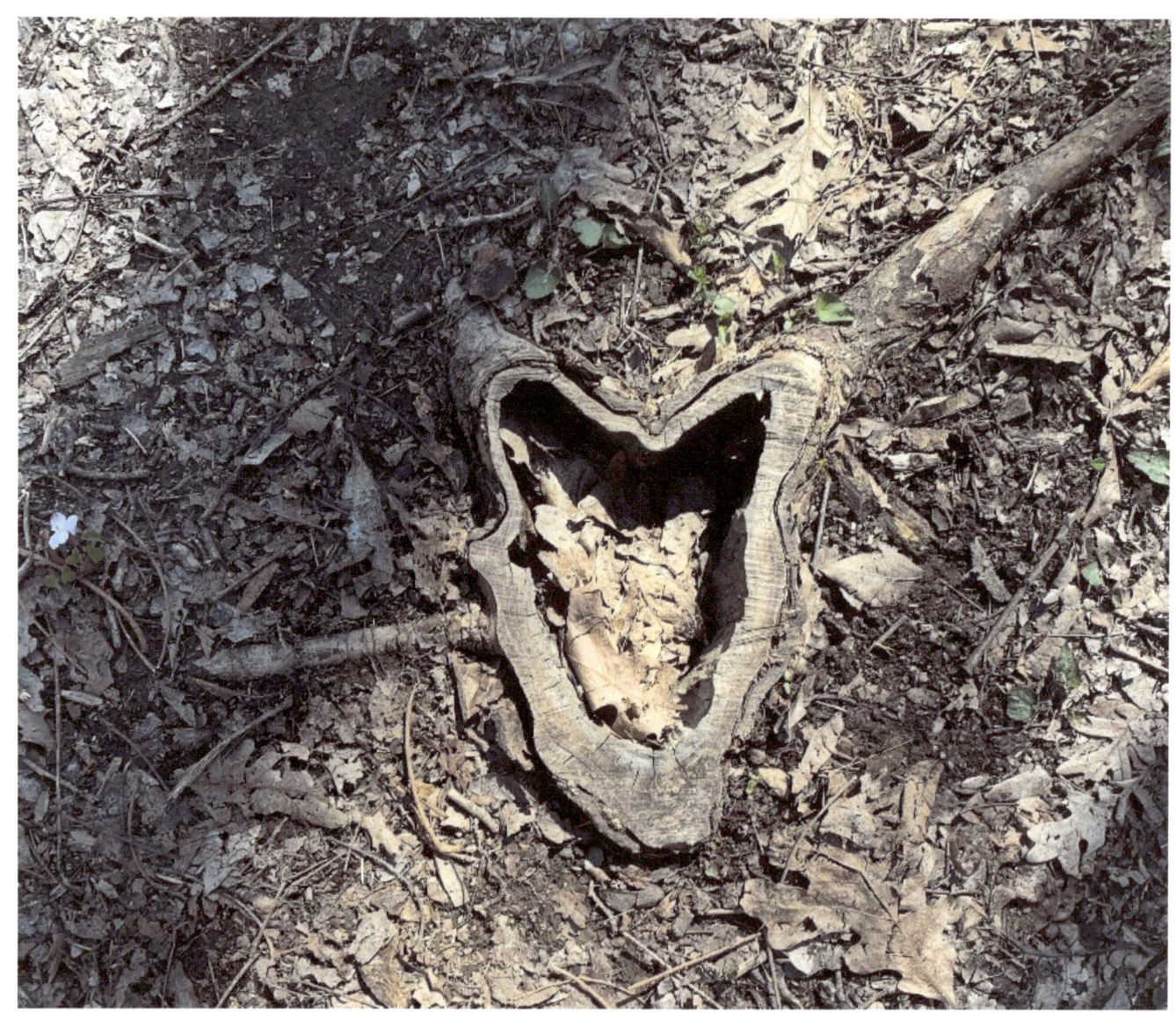

TREE STUMP

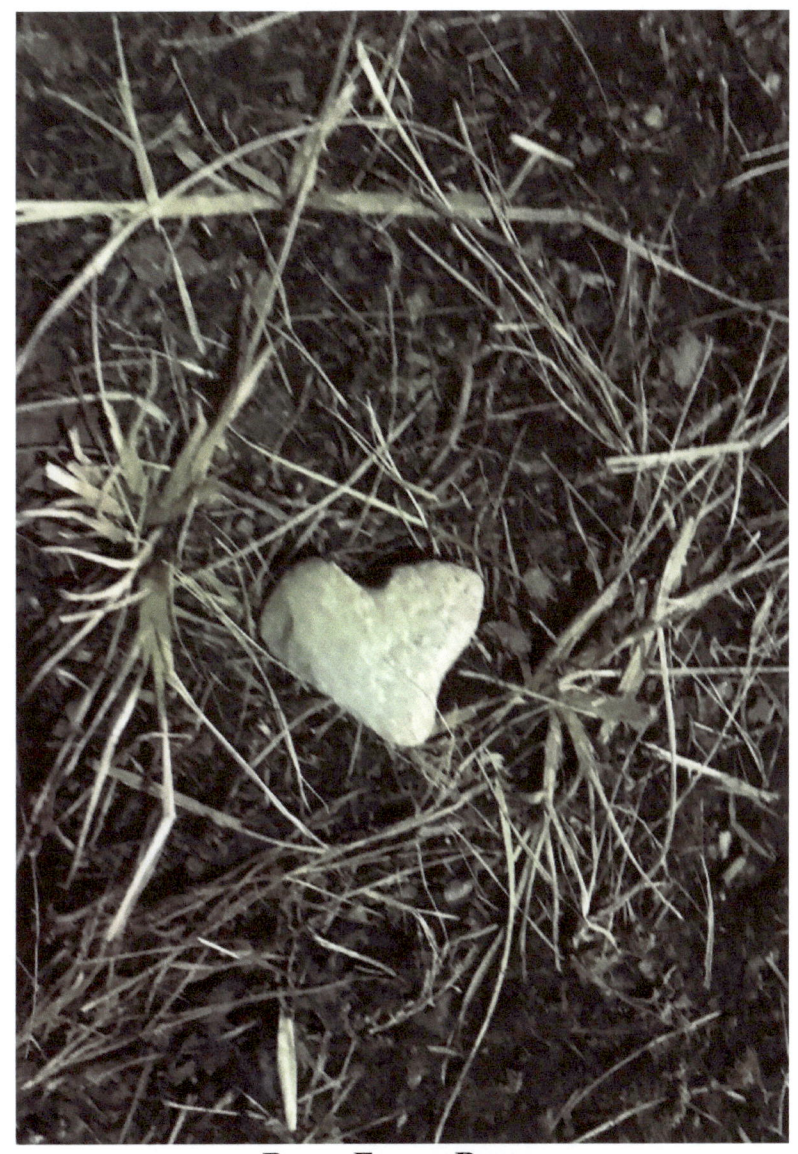

BALL FIELD ROCK

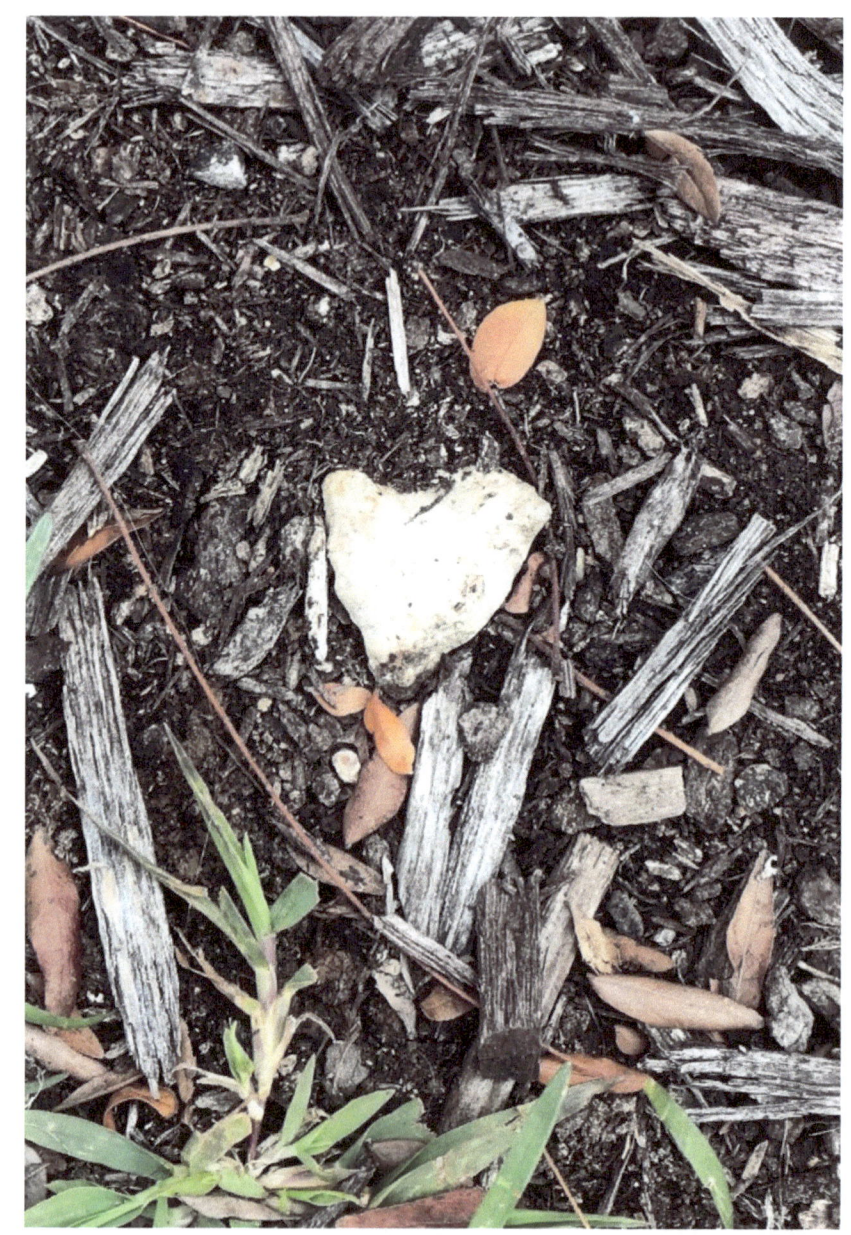

BASEBALL FIELD FIND

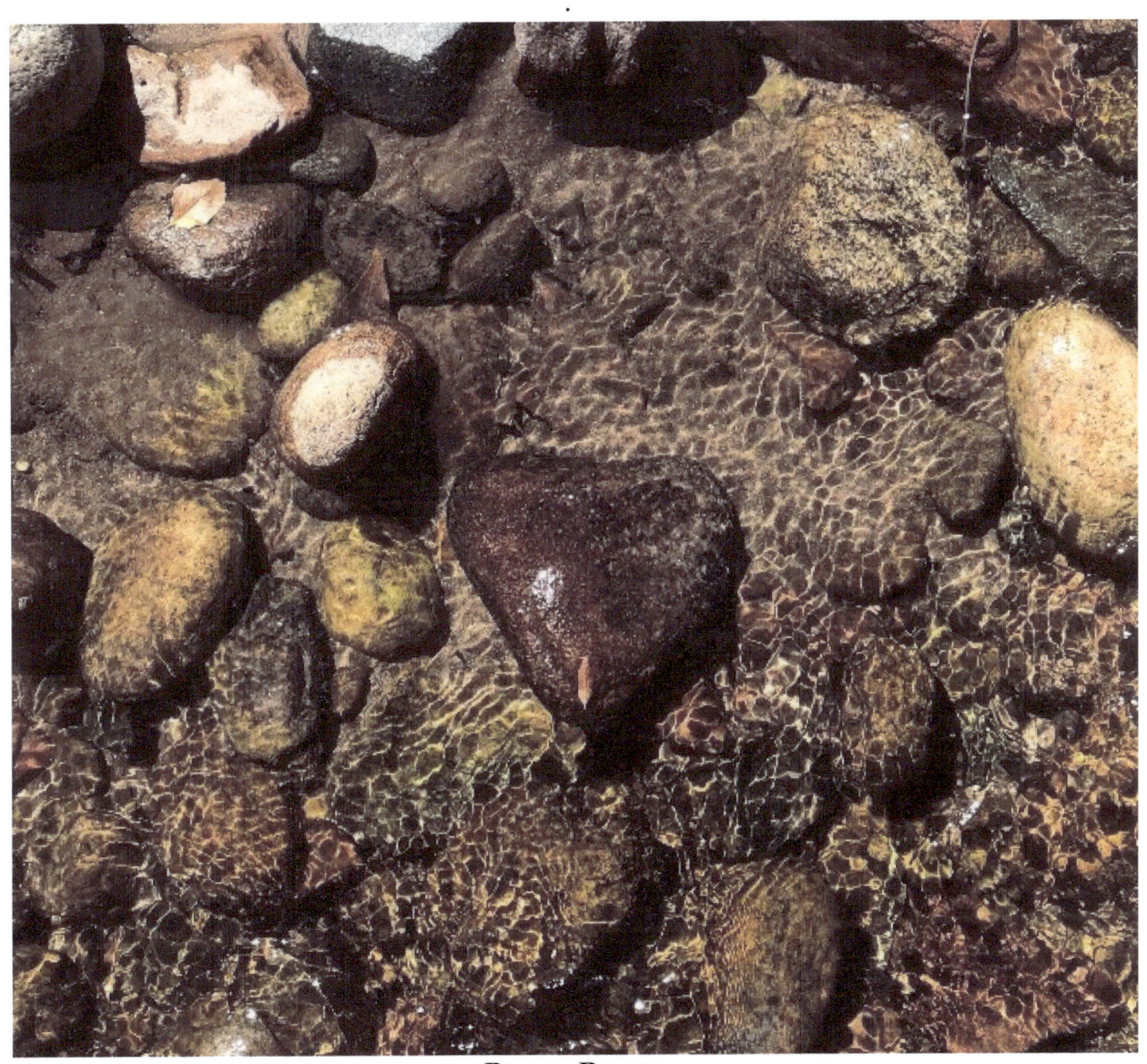

RIVER ROCK

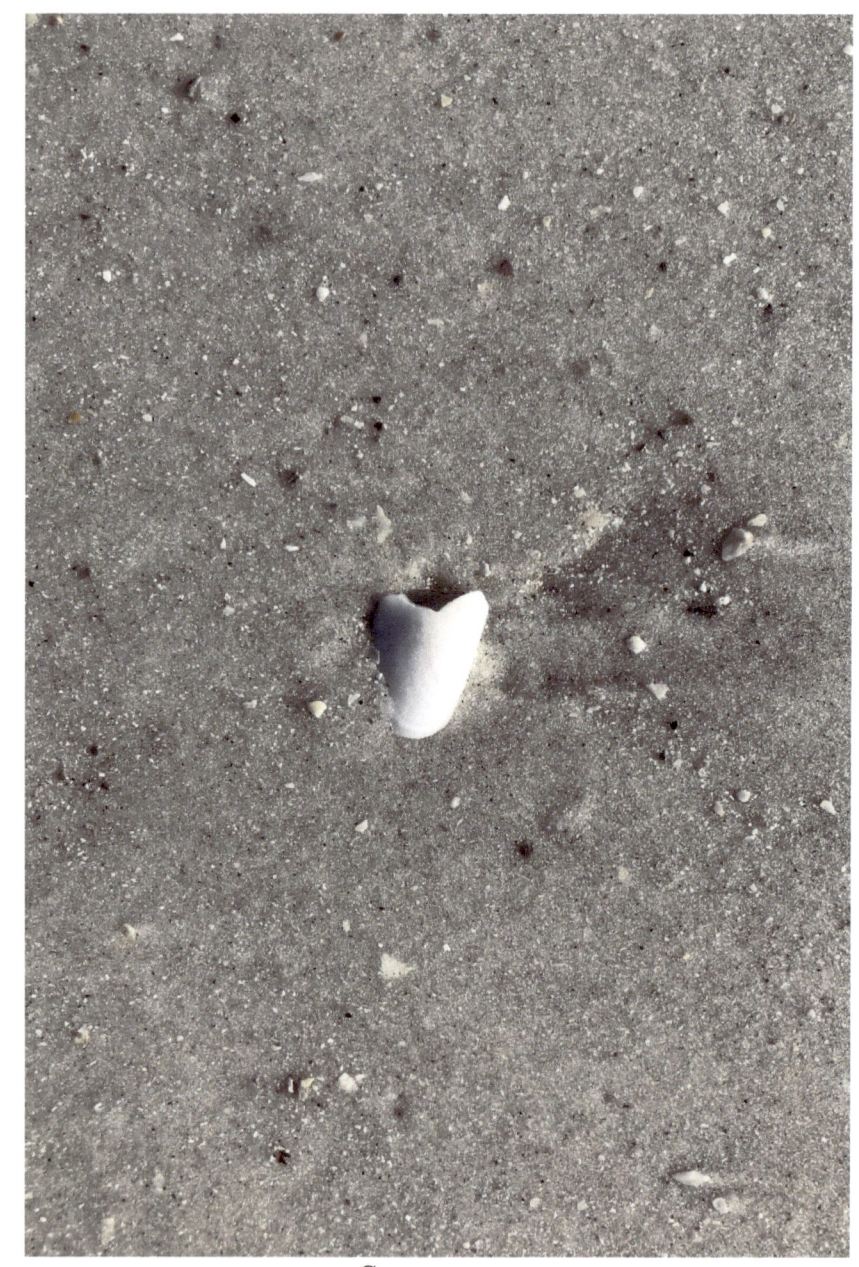

SEASHELL

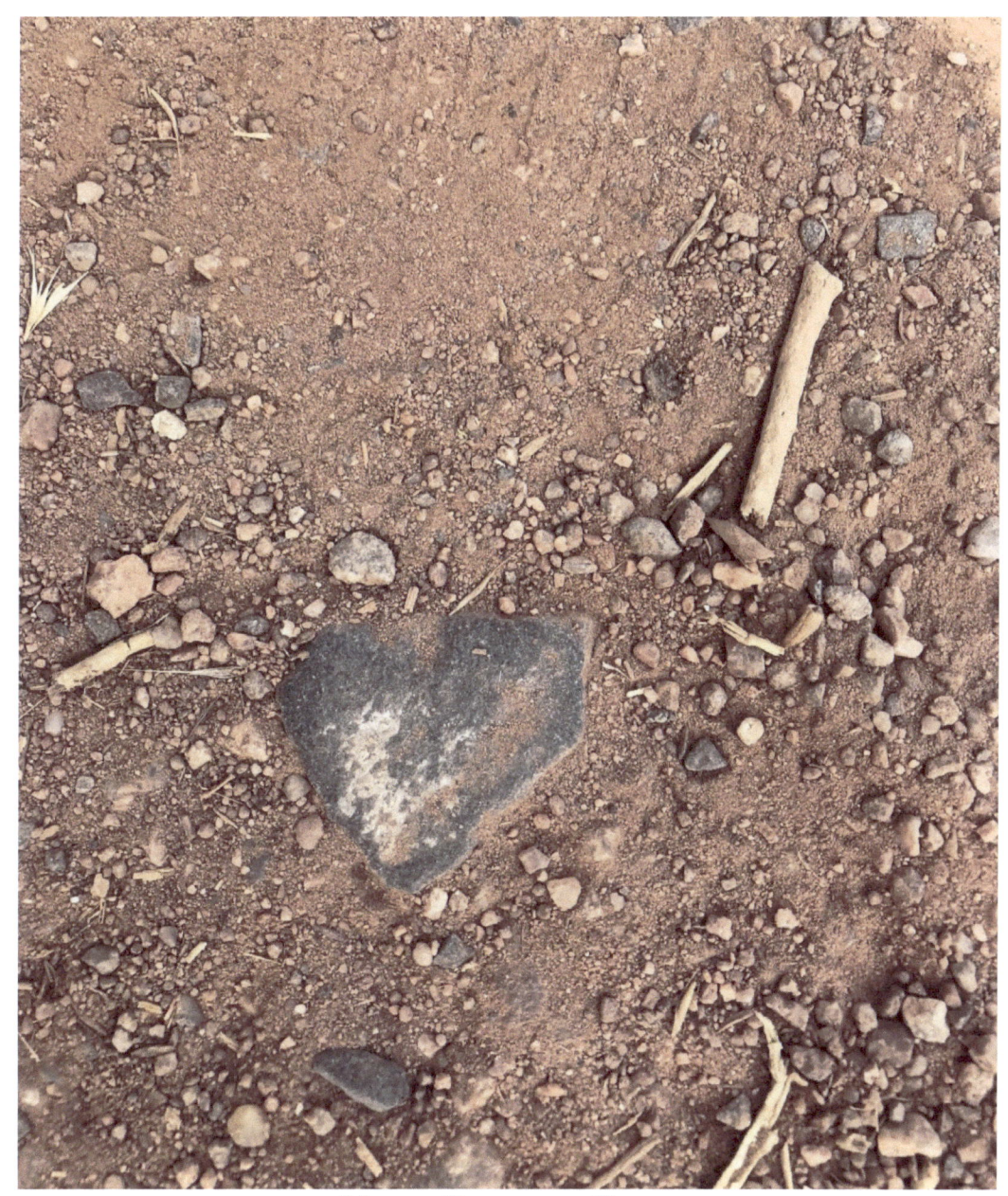
MUSIC FESTIVAL ROCK

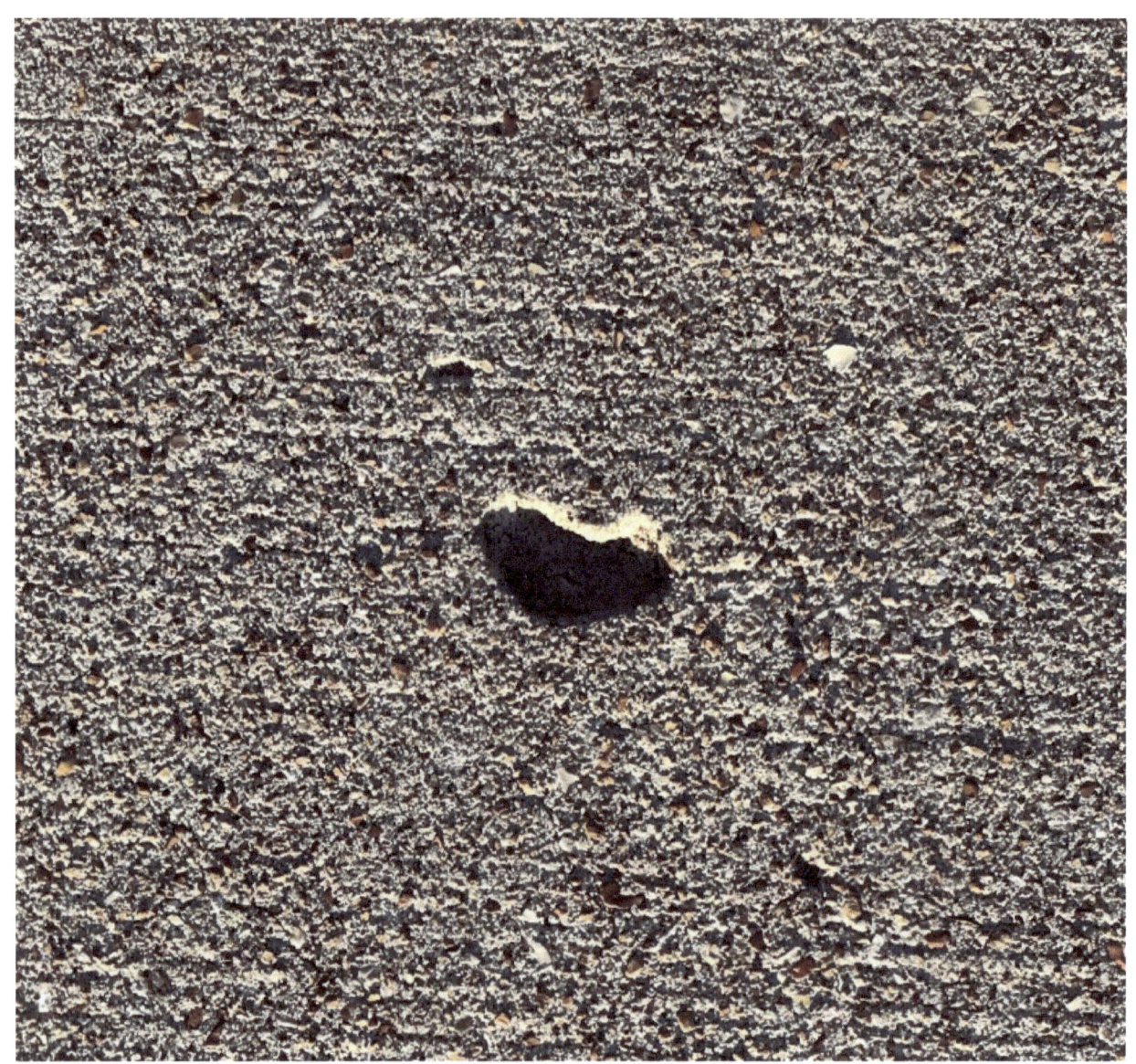

CHUNK OUT OF SIDEWALK

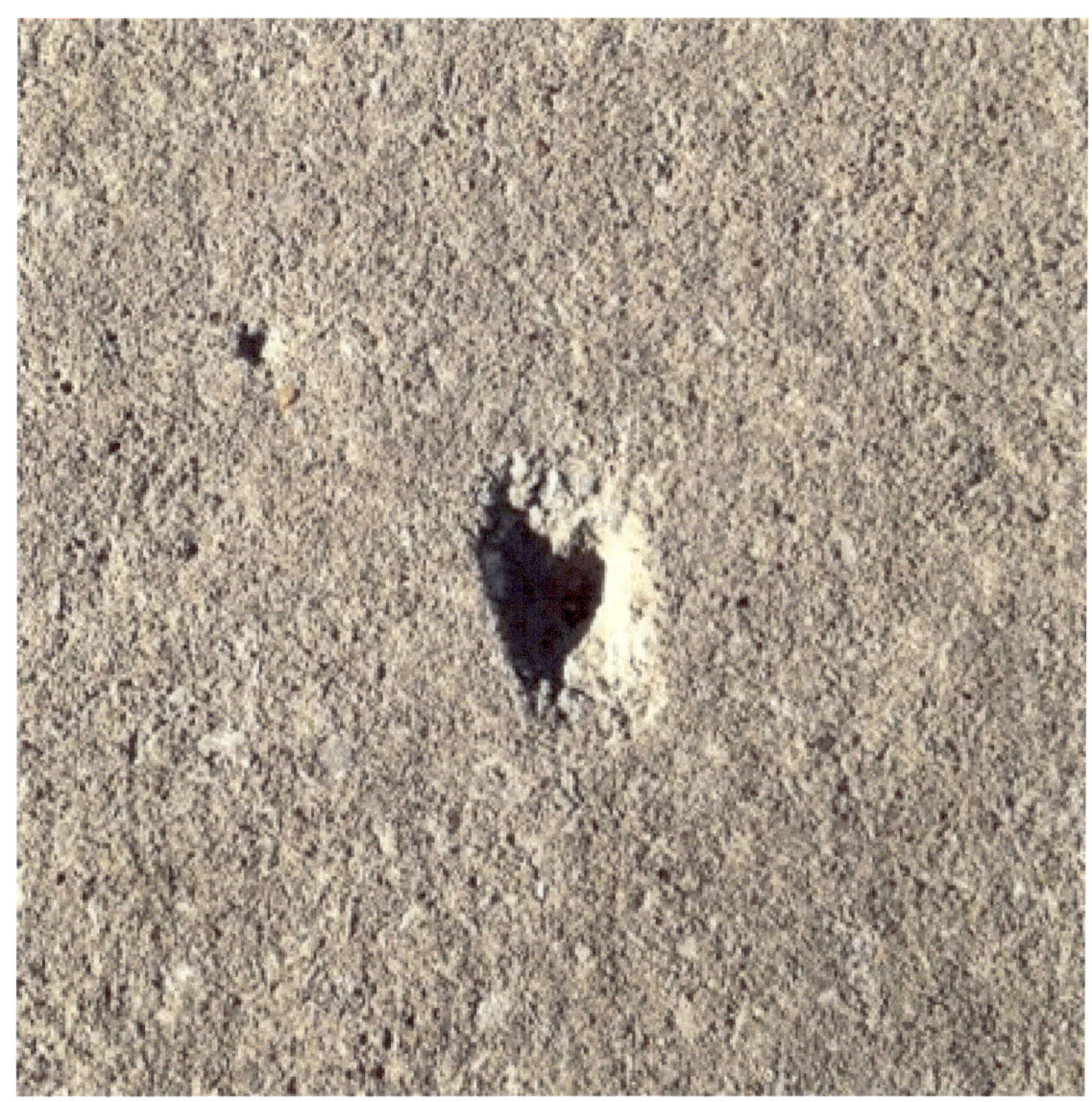
Another Chunk out of Sidewalk

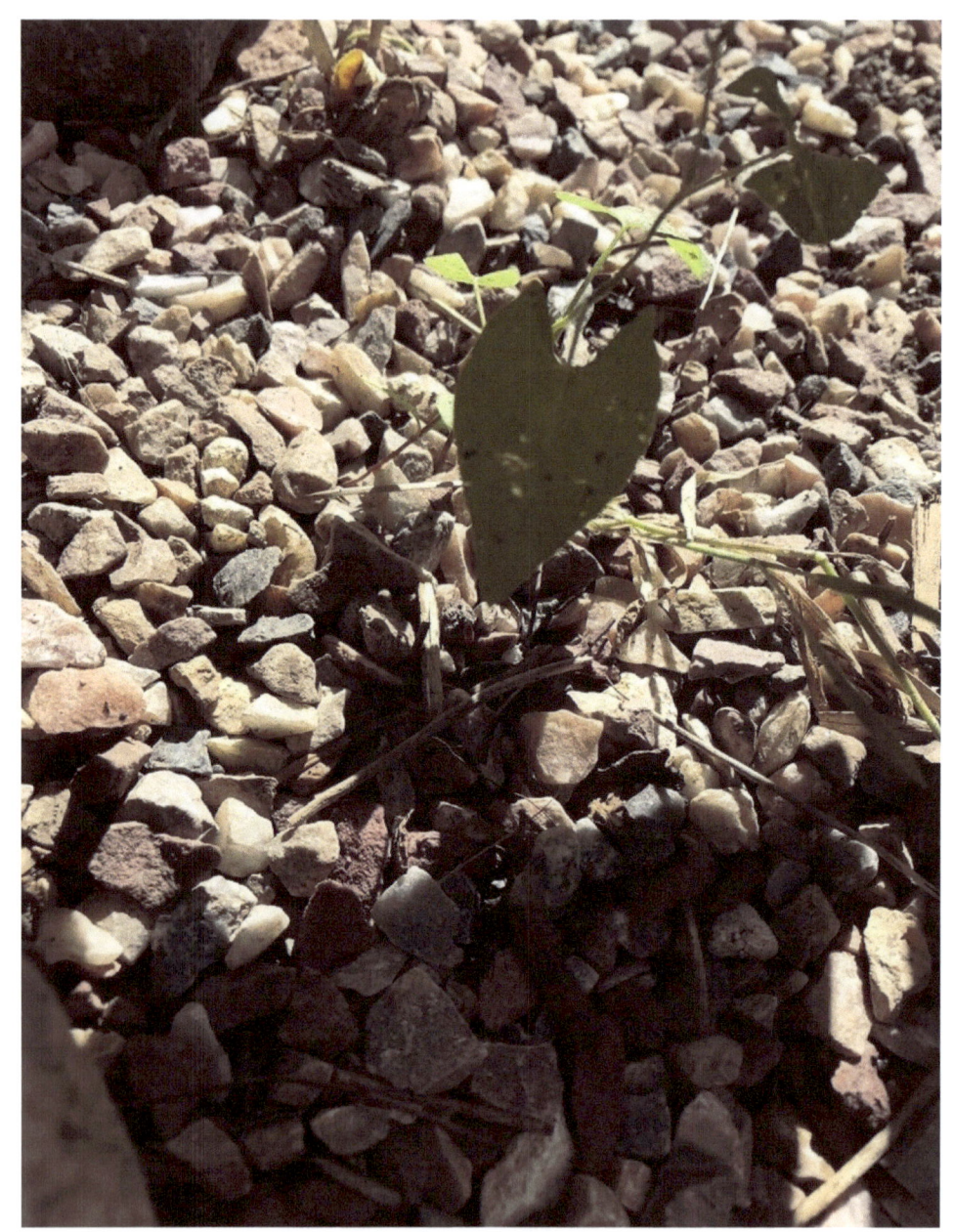

AMONG THE ROCKS

STREETS, SIDEWALKS, DRIVEWAYS & FLOORS

DIRT...

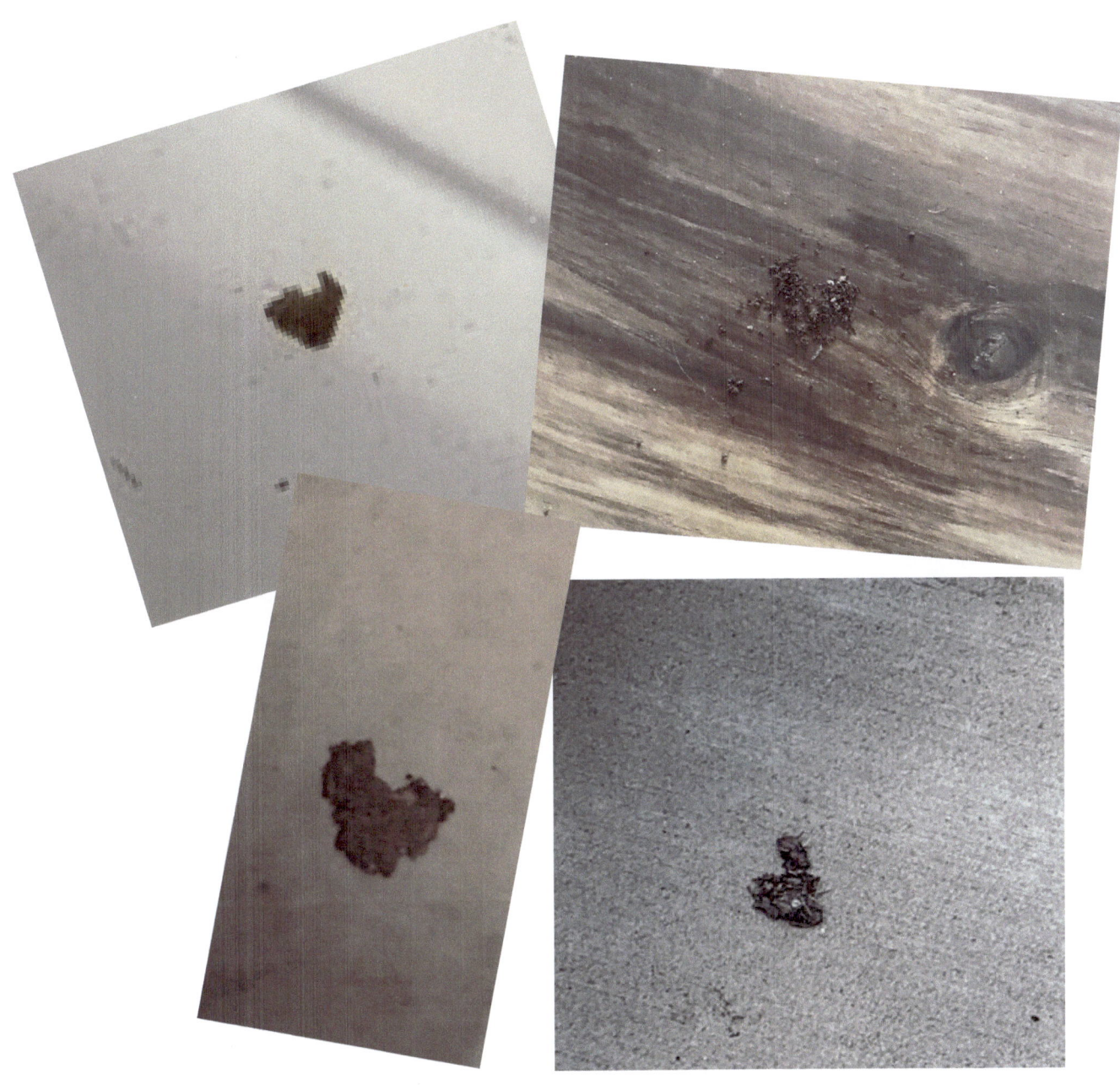

GUM…

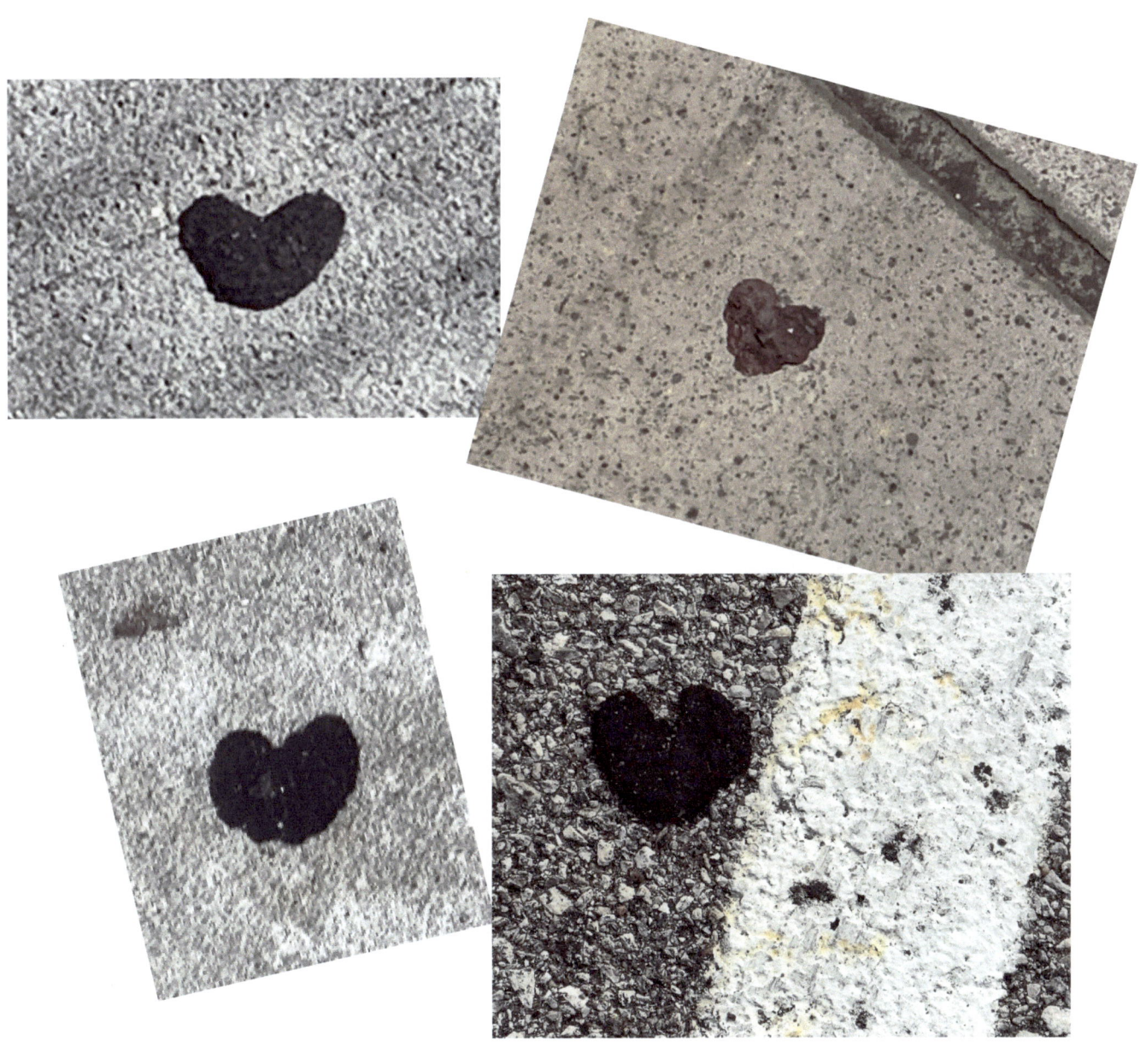

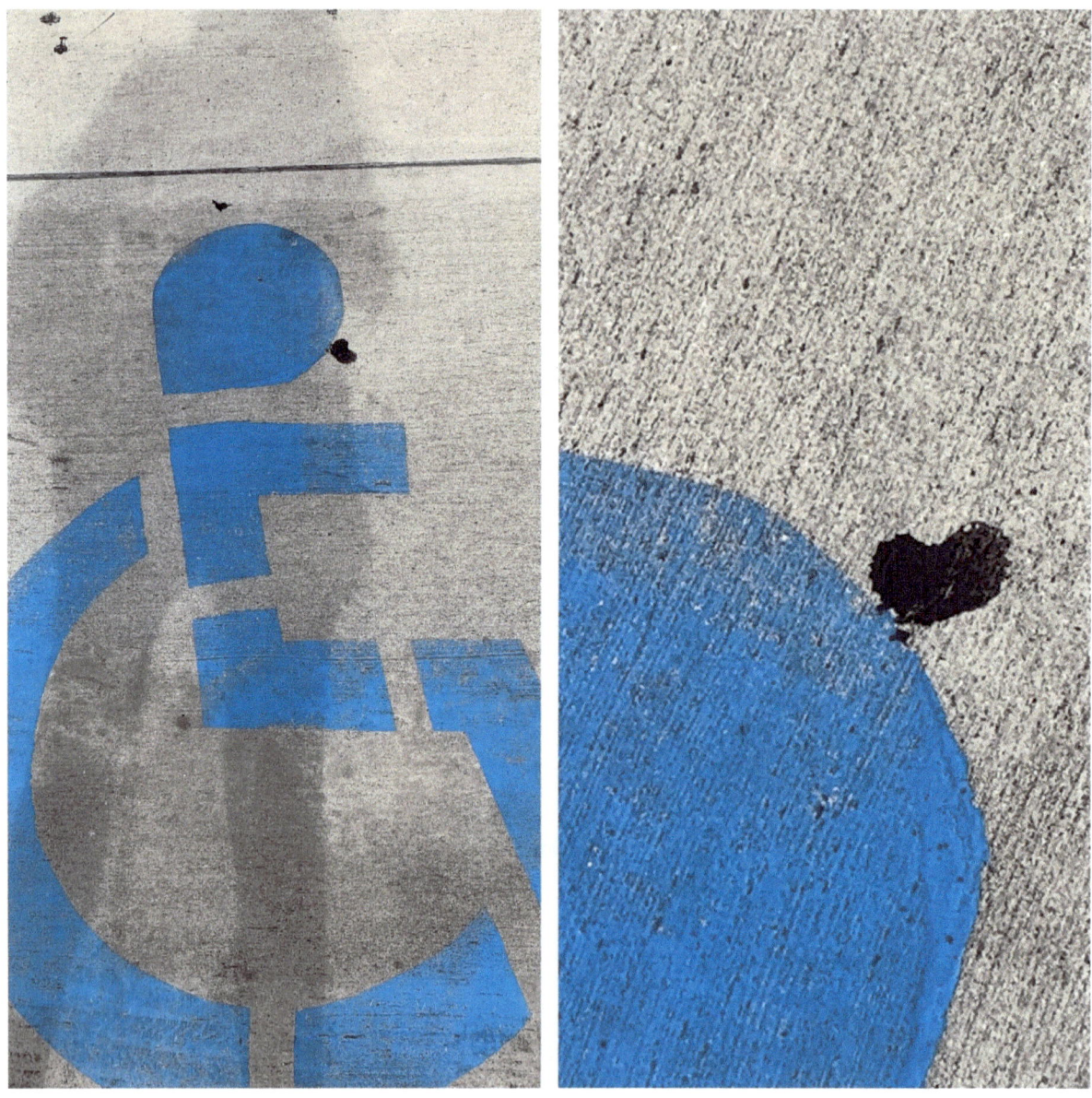

LEAVES…

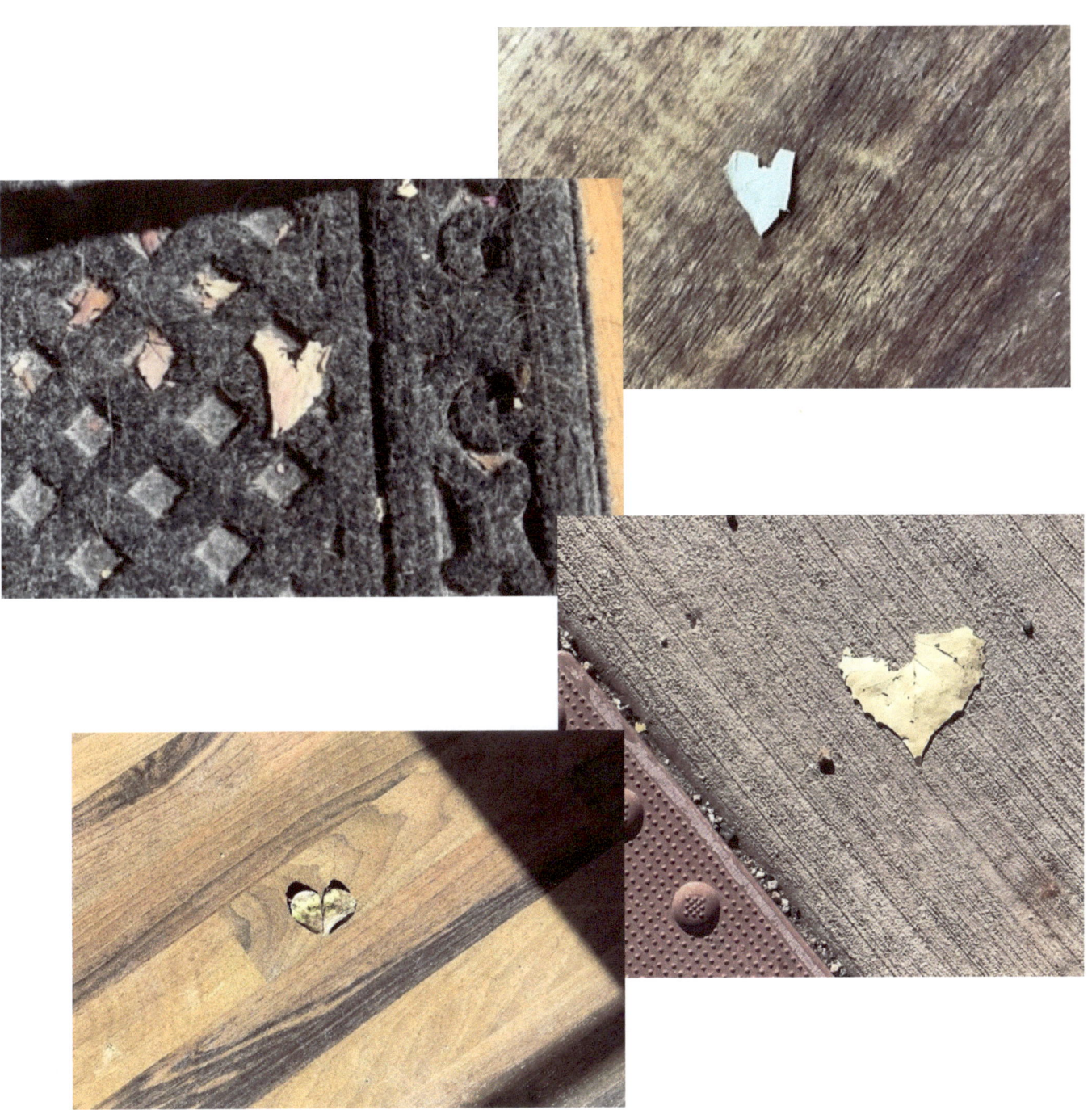

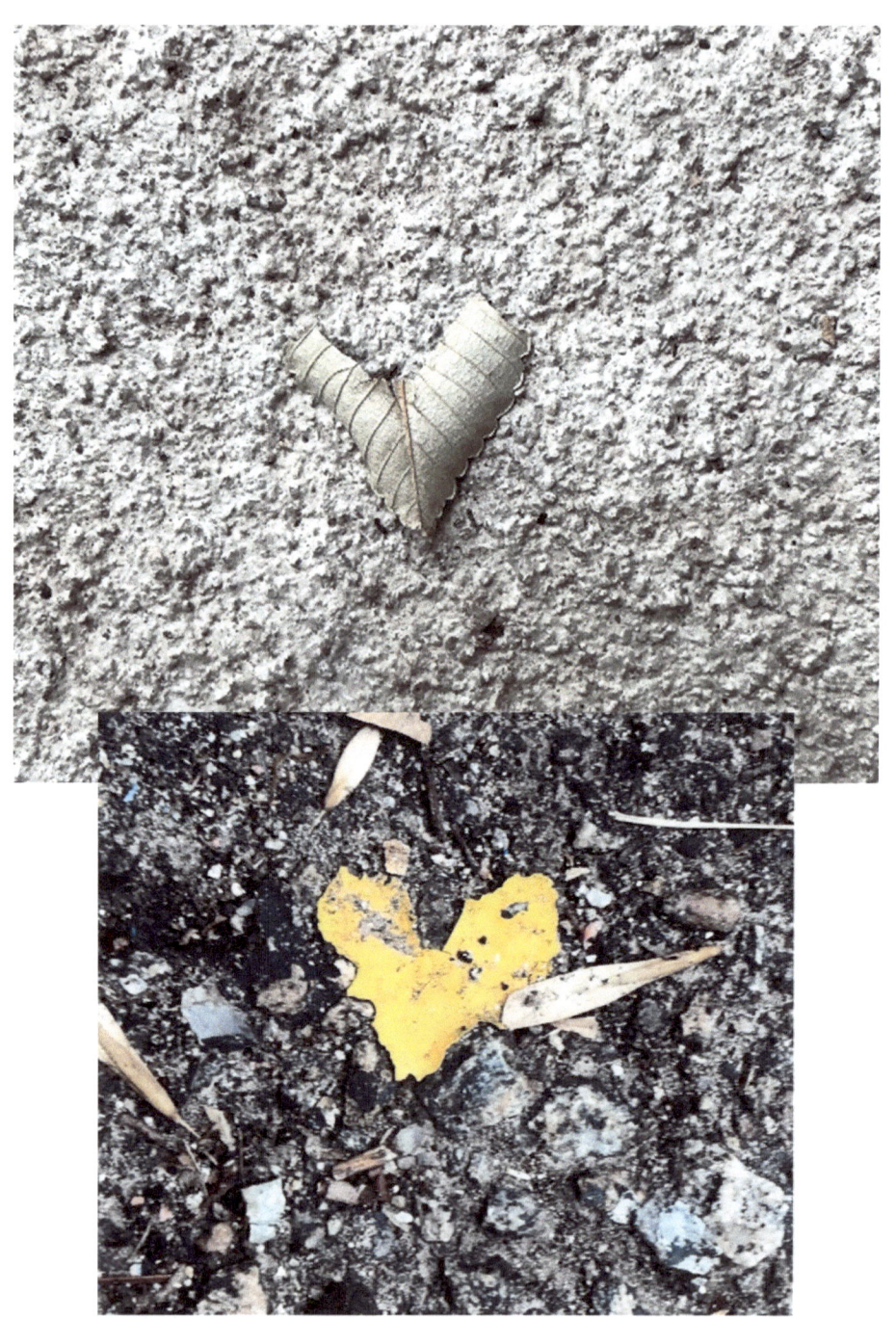

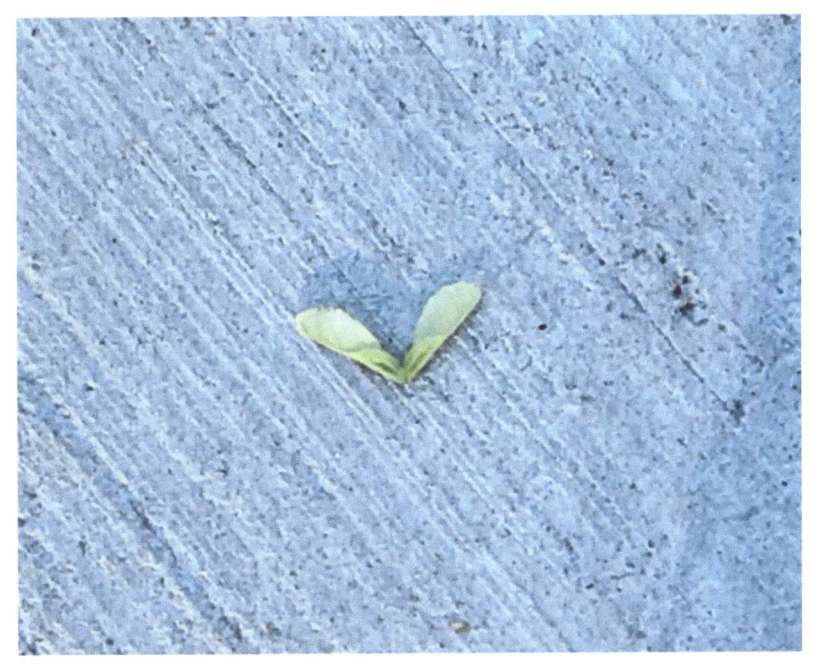
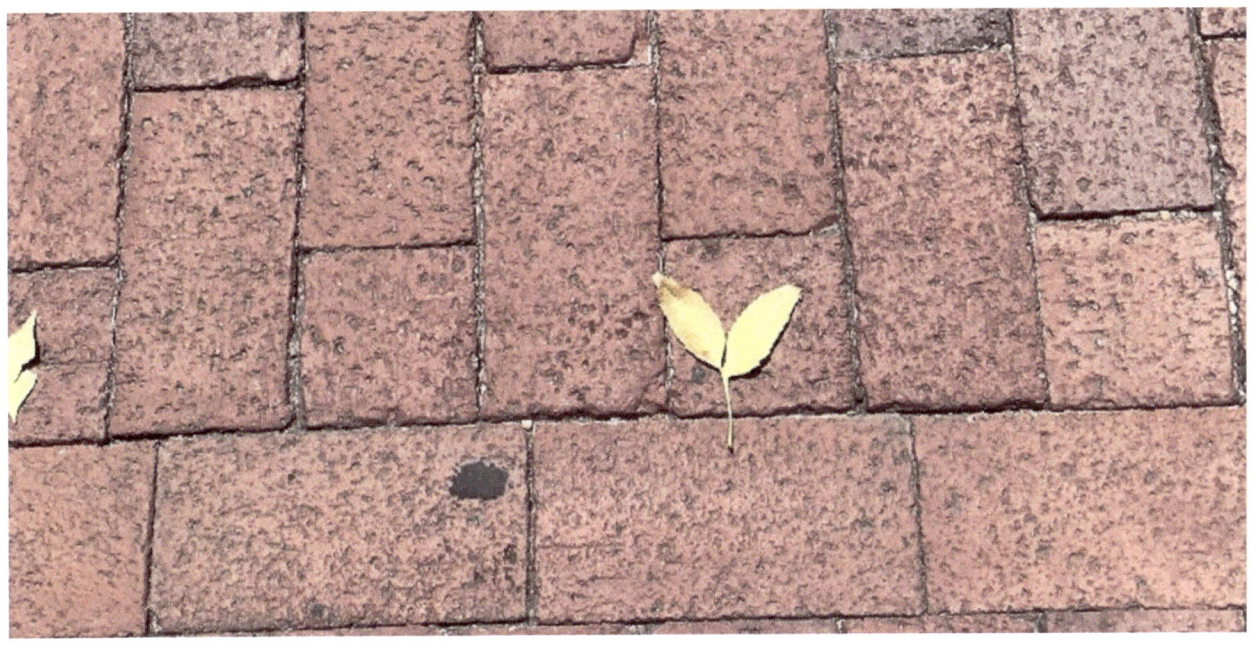

PAINT…

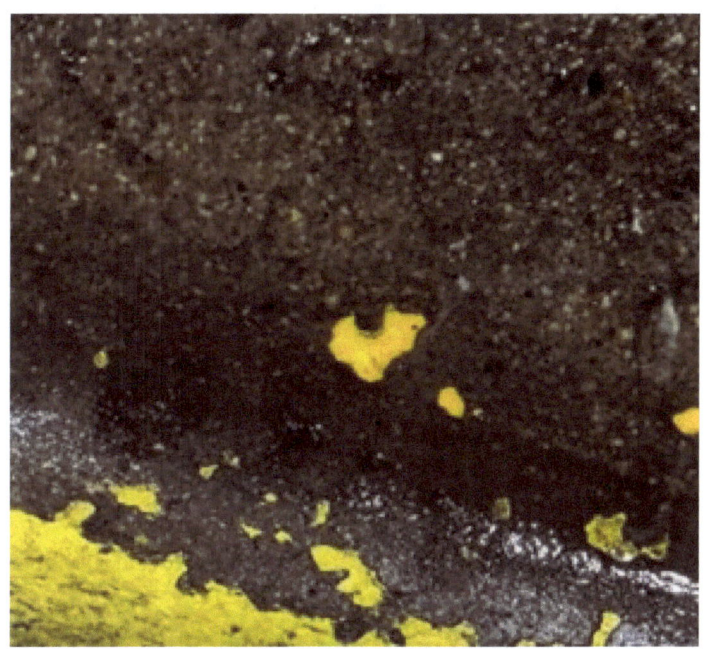
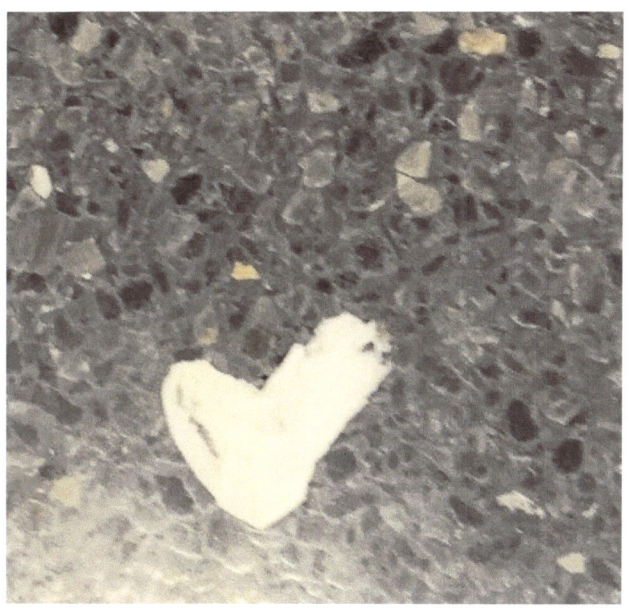
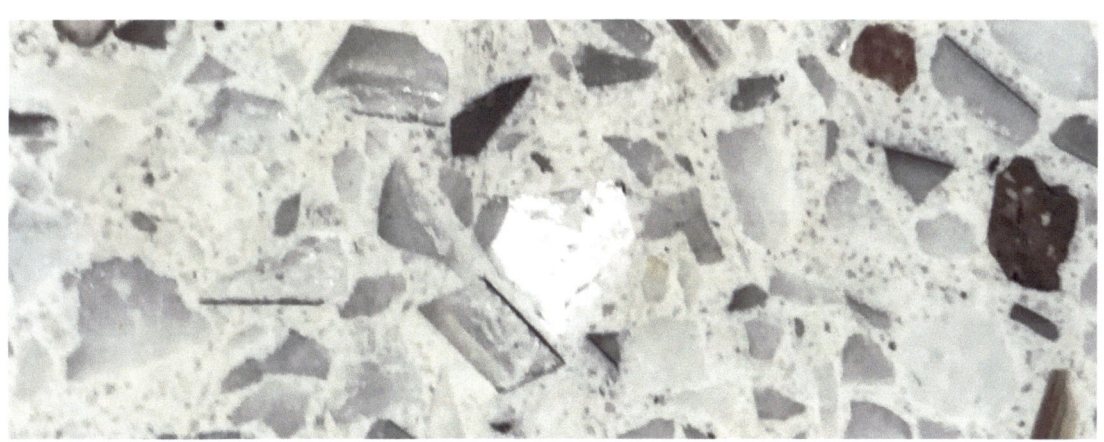

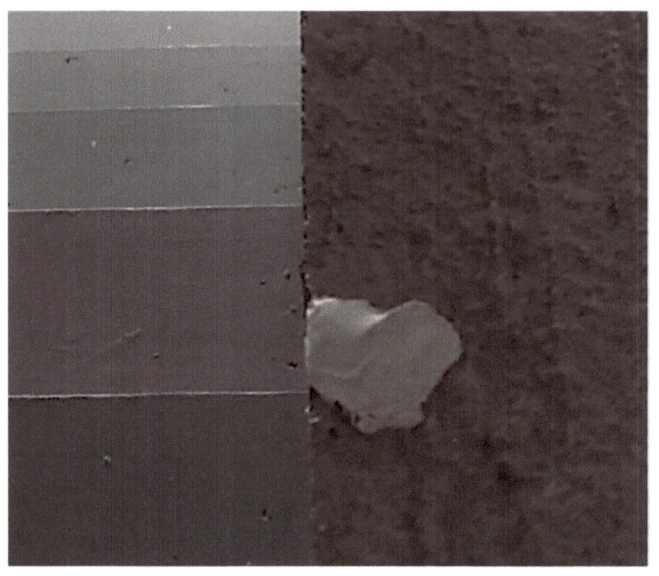
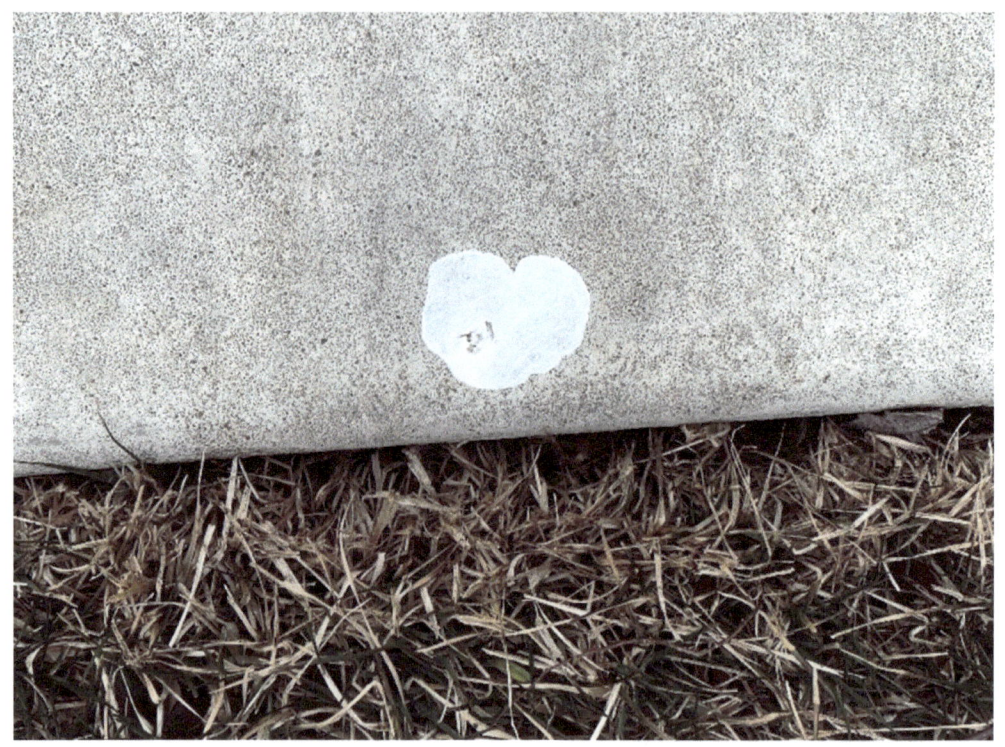

STAINS…

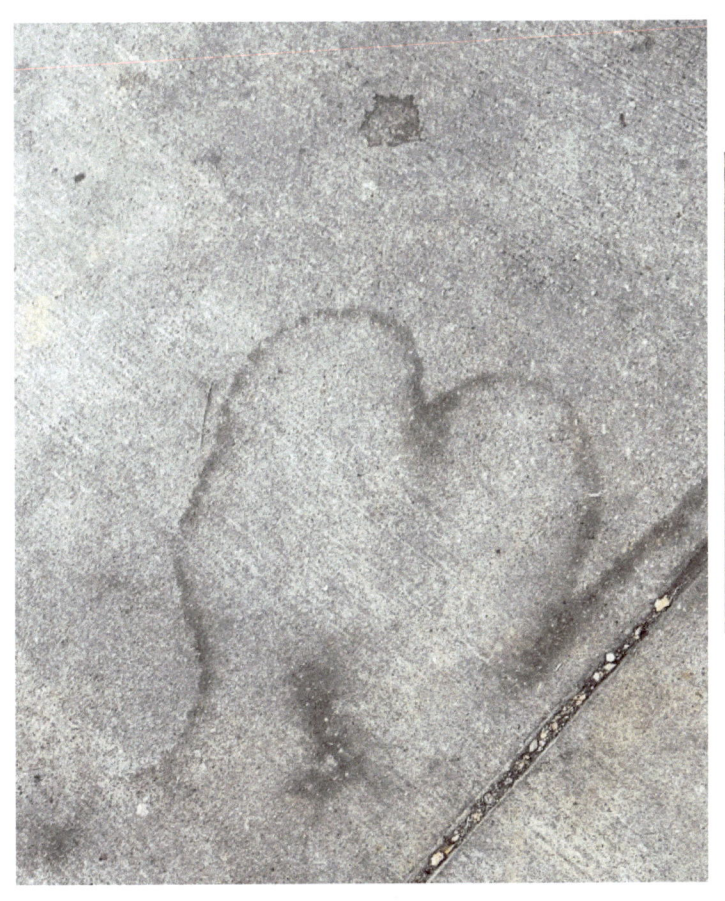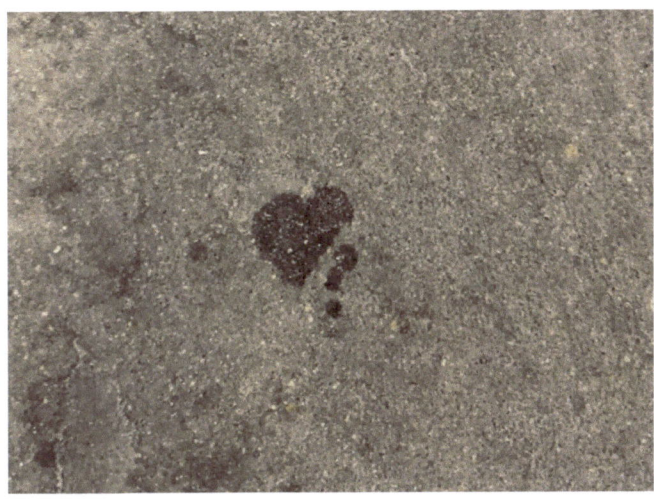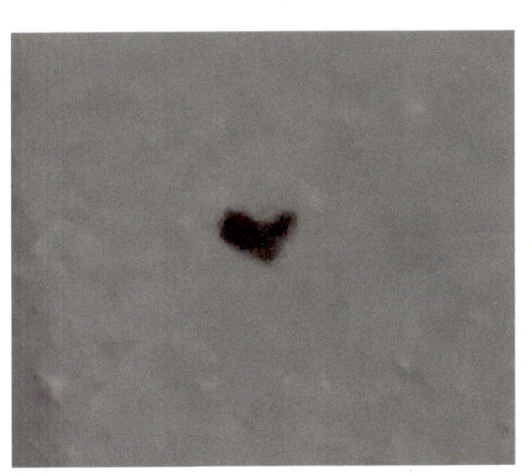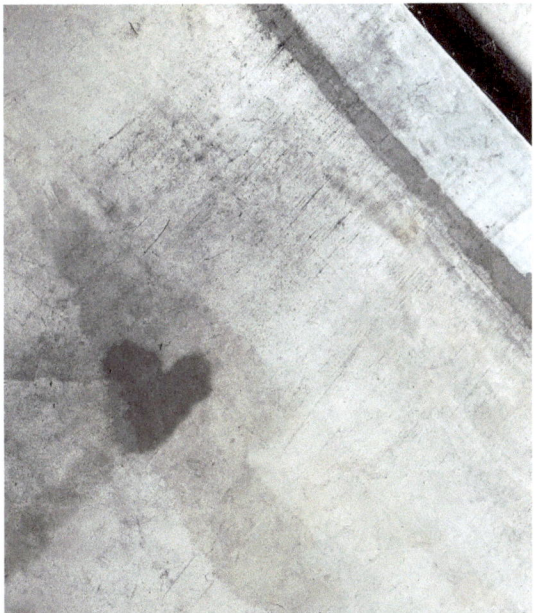

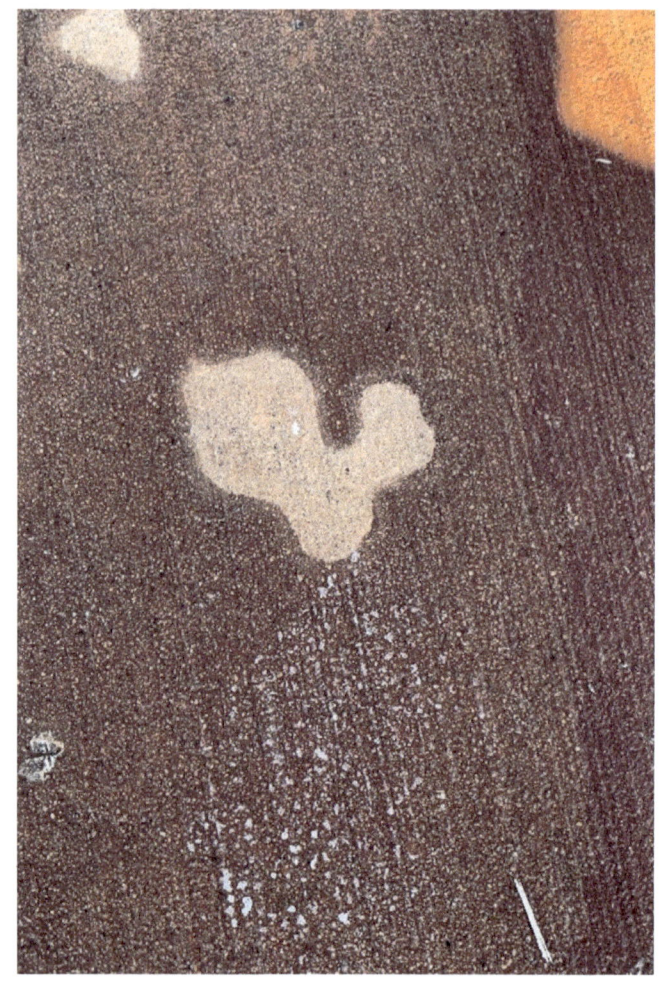
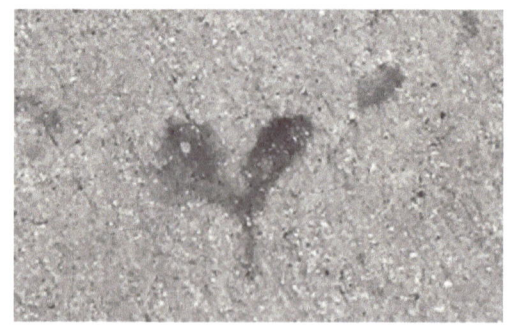

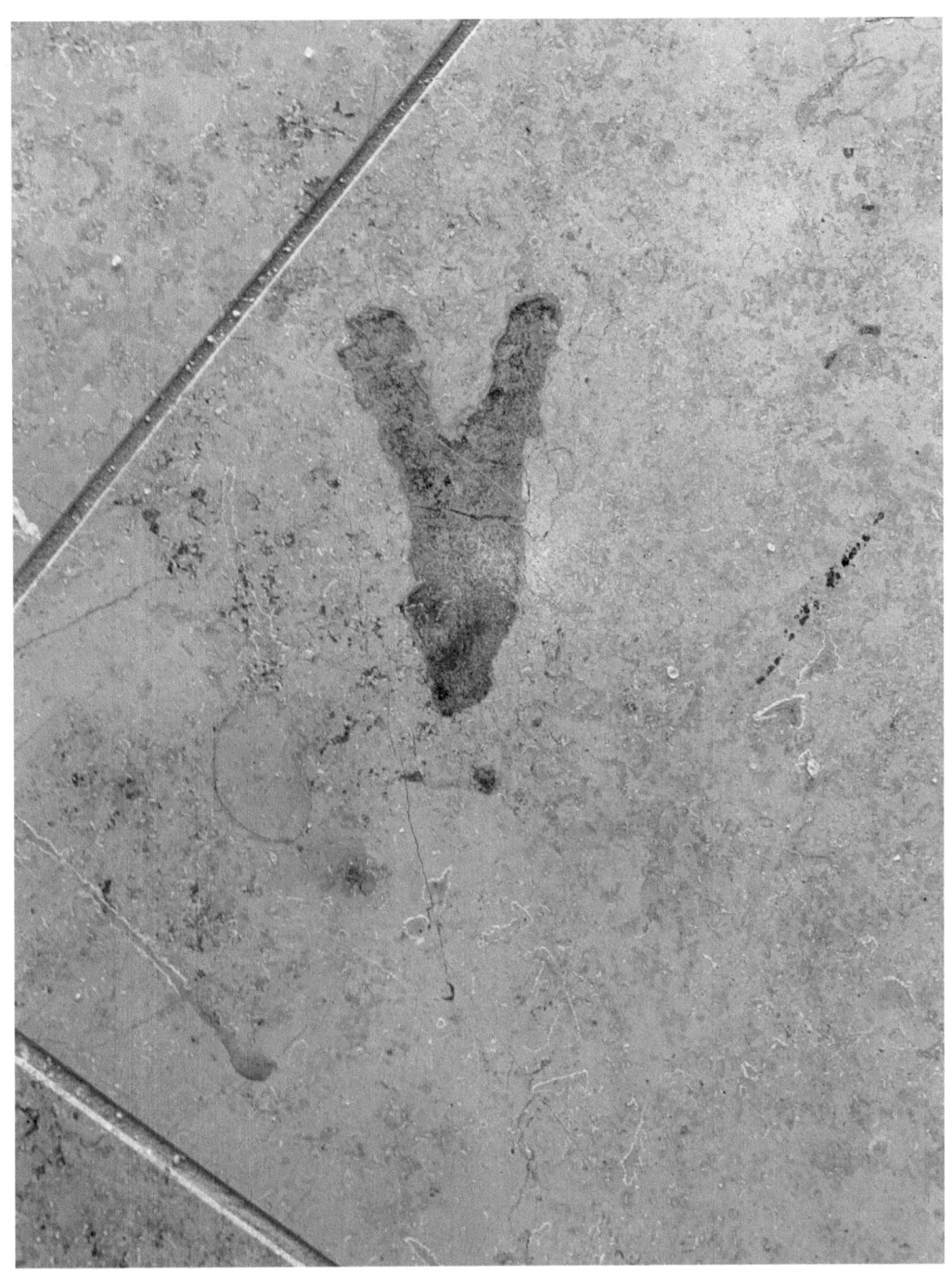

Food

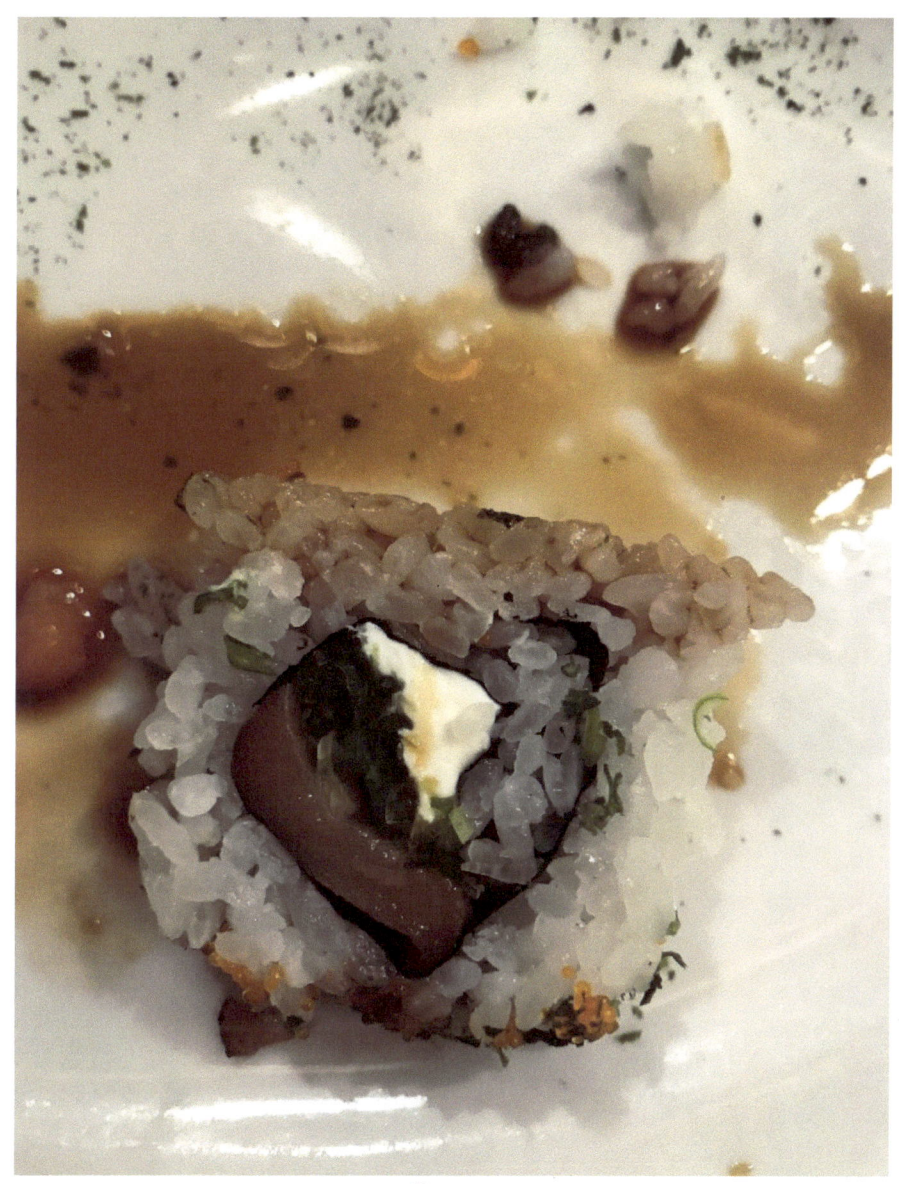

SUSHI

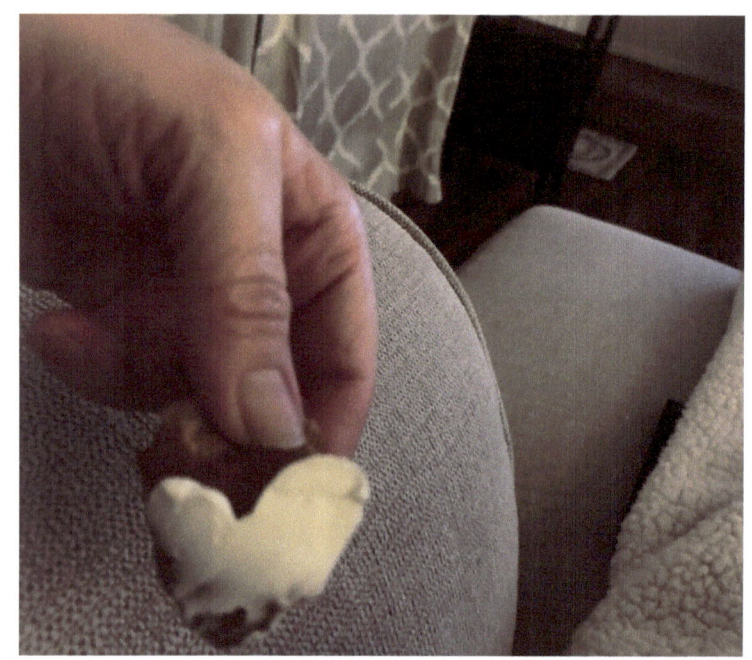
CREAM CHEESE SWIPE

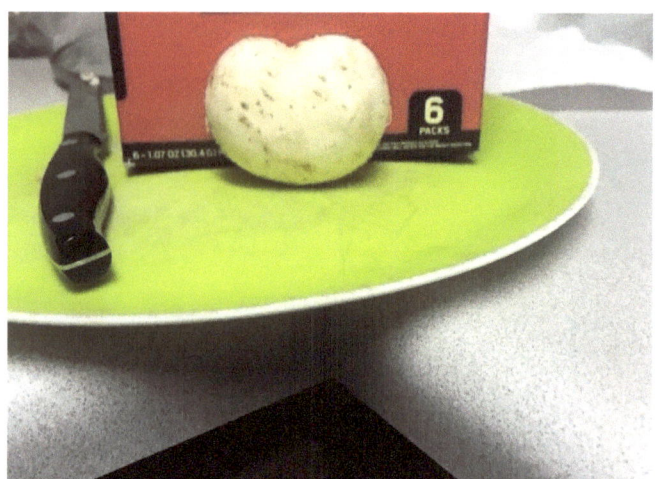
MUSHROOM

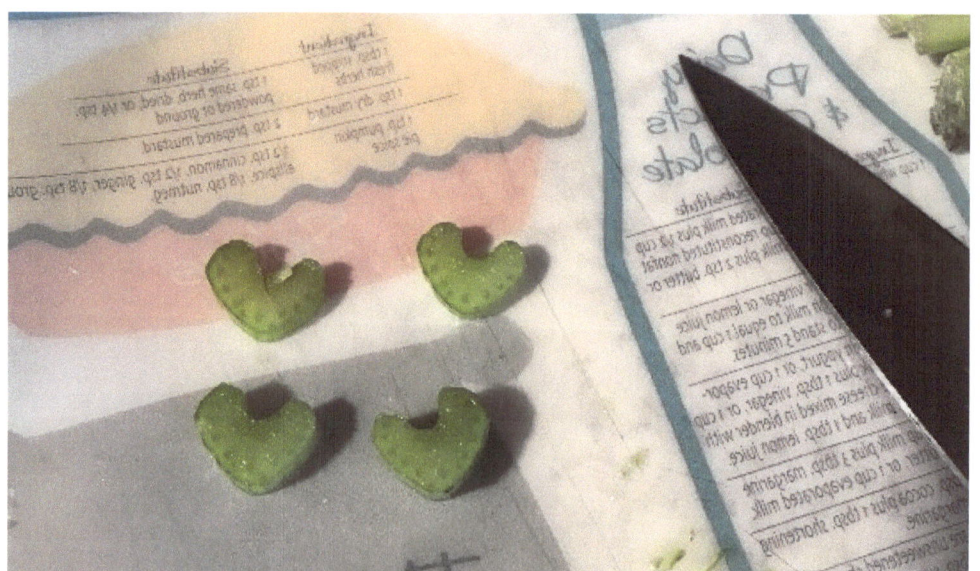
CHOPPED CELERY

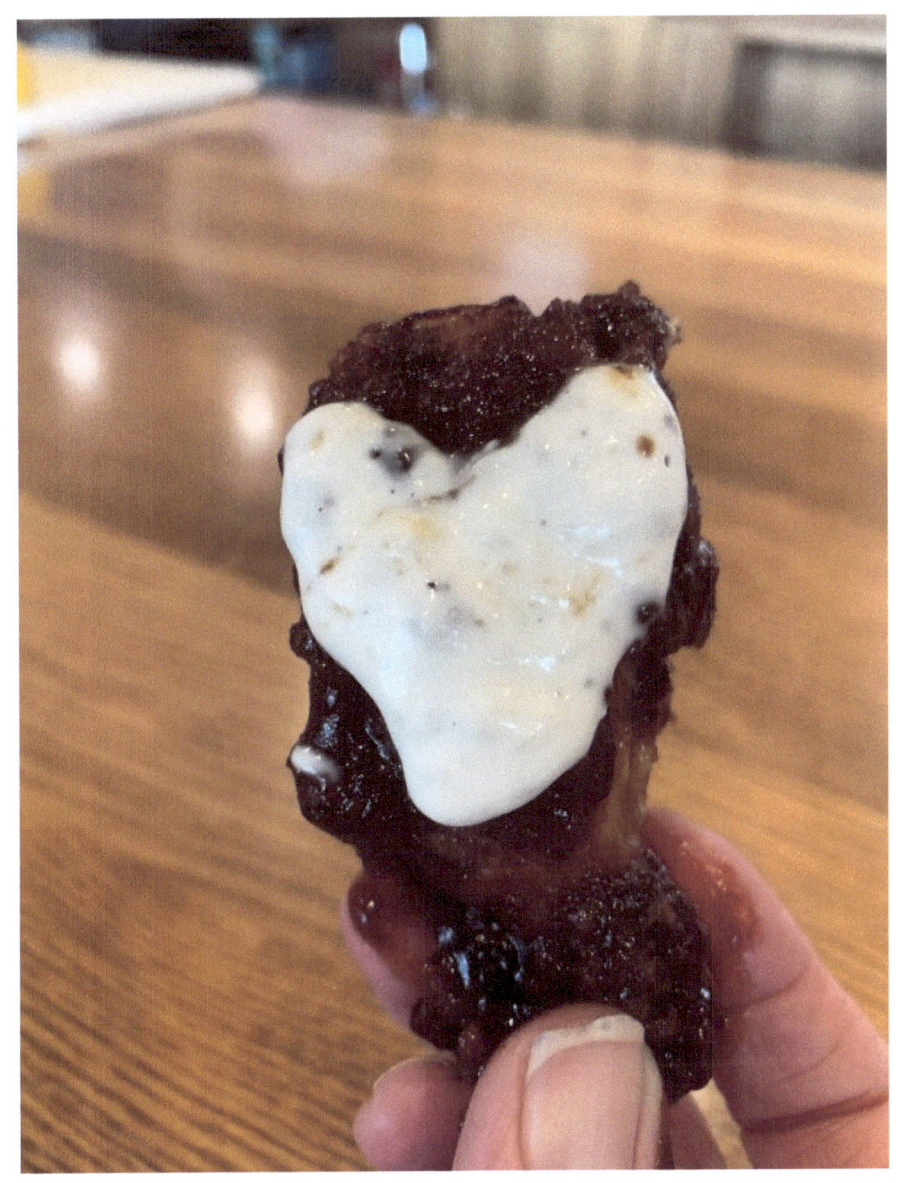

BLUE CHEESE DRESSING SWIPE

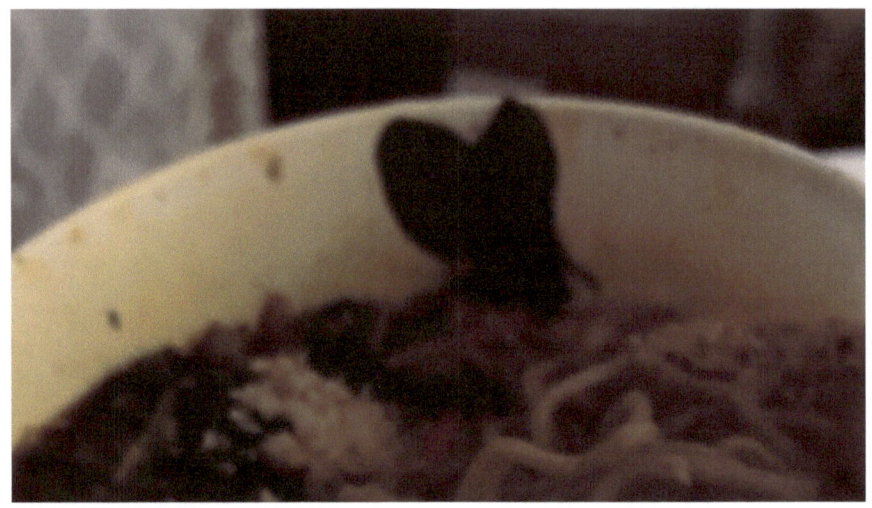

Spinach

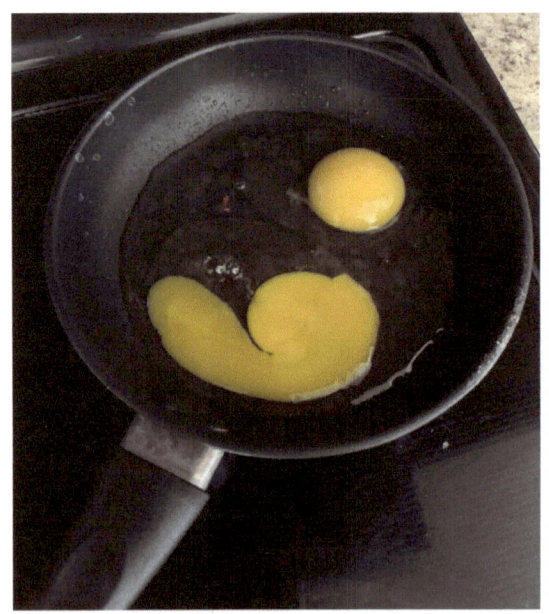

Broken Egg Yolk

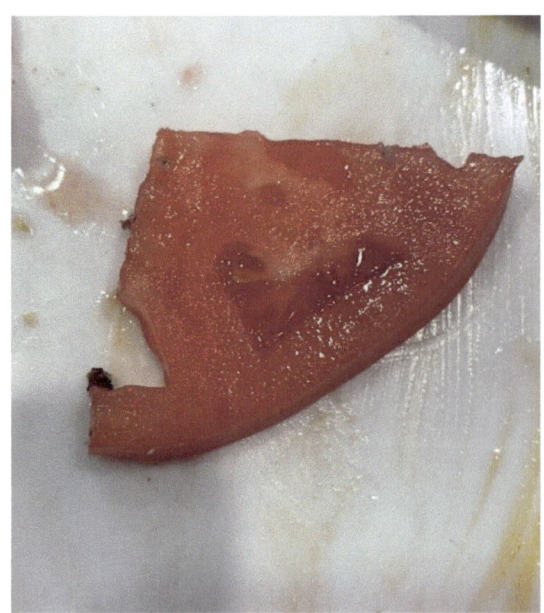

Tomato

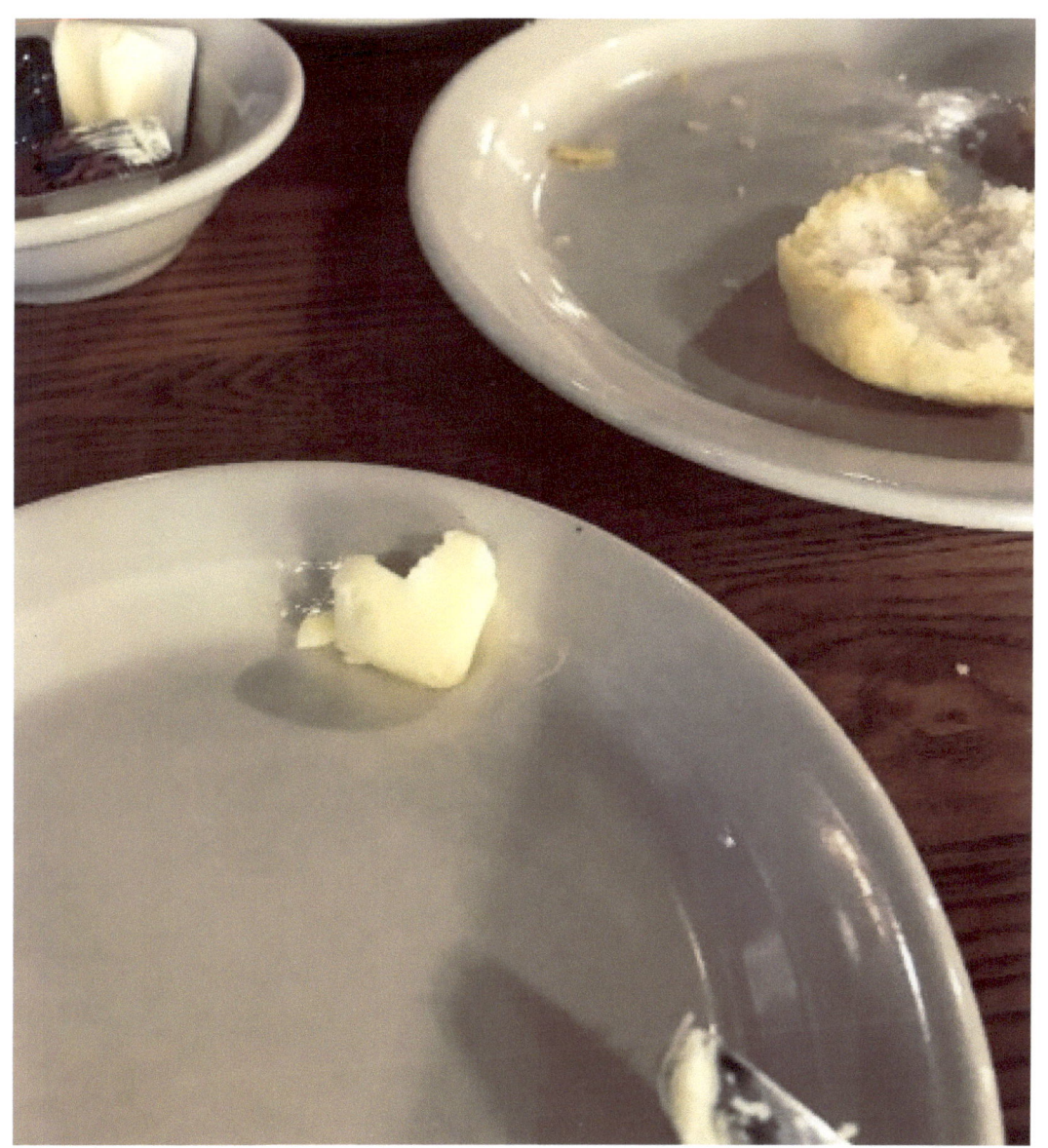

BUTTER SWIPE

Chicken Breast

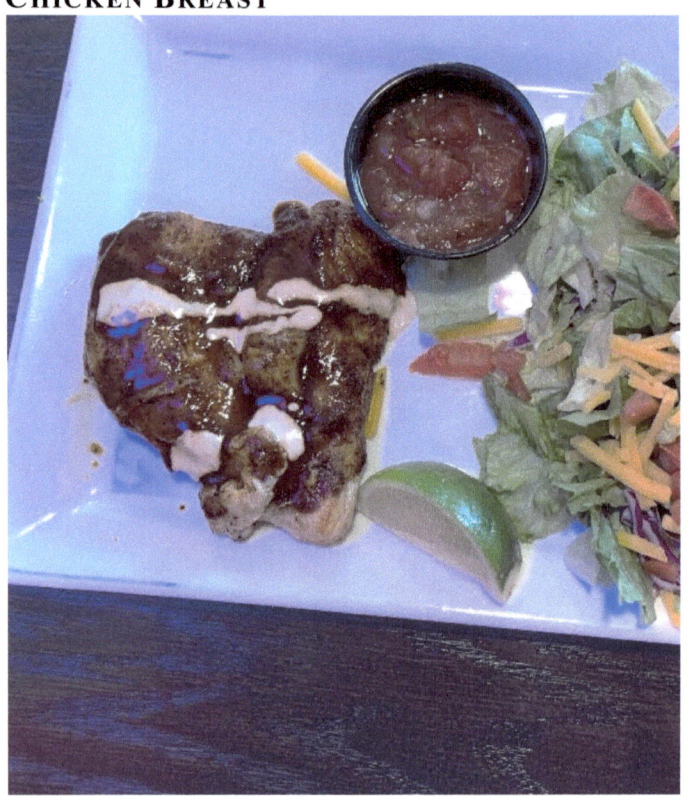

Dried Fruit

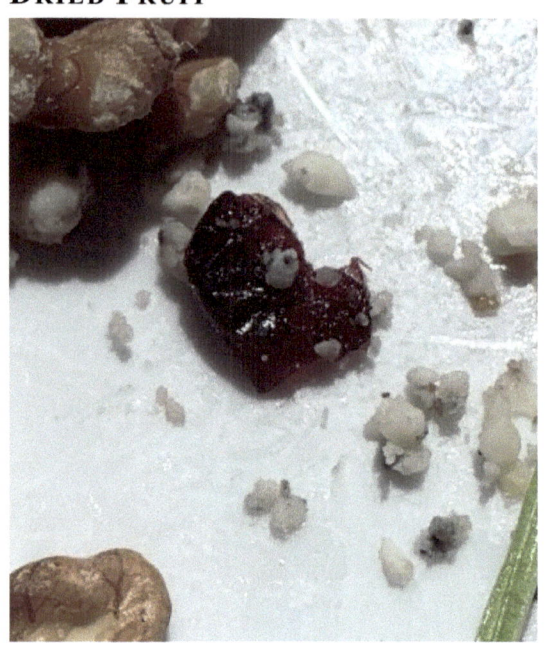

Lemonade Spill

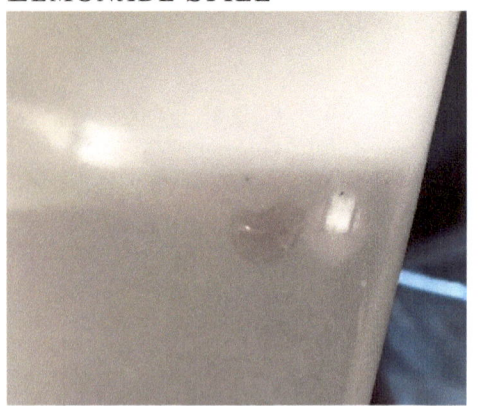

Bacon & Eggs

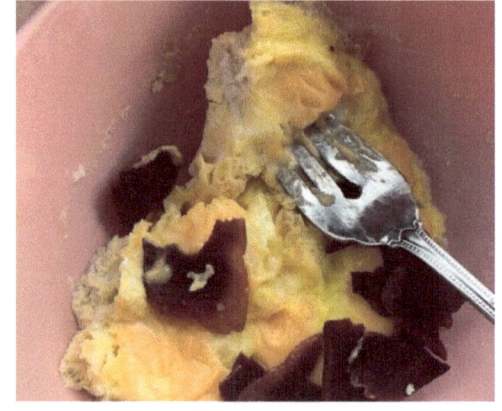

Cookie Dough Ice Cream x2

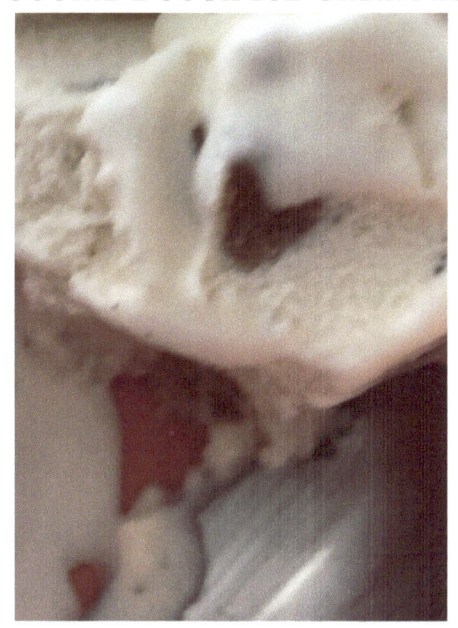

Sliced Carrot

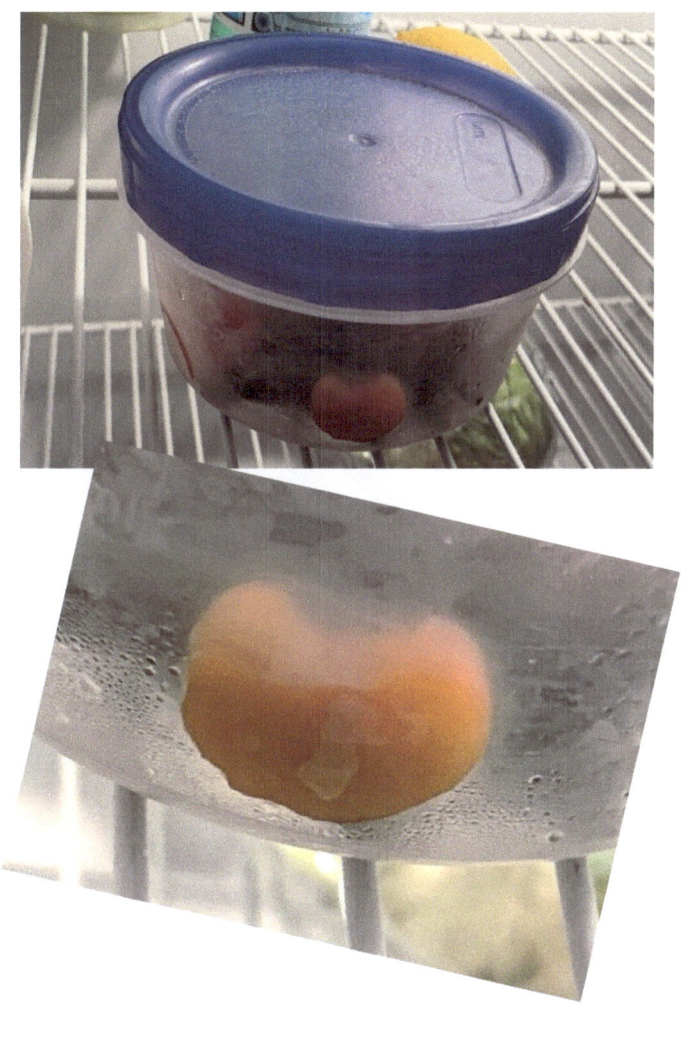

Burnt Pop Tart

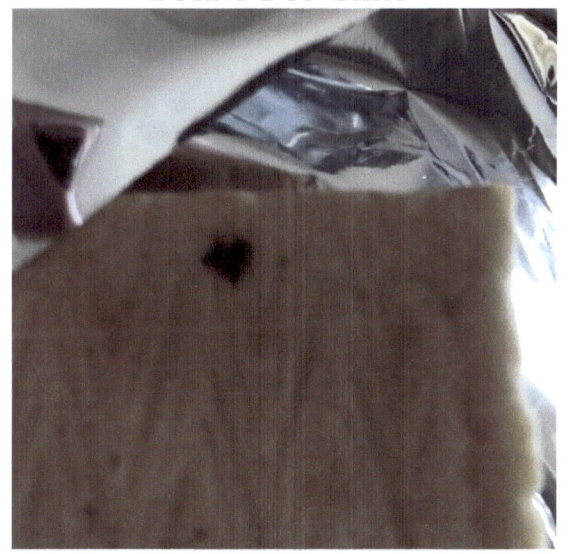

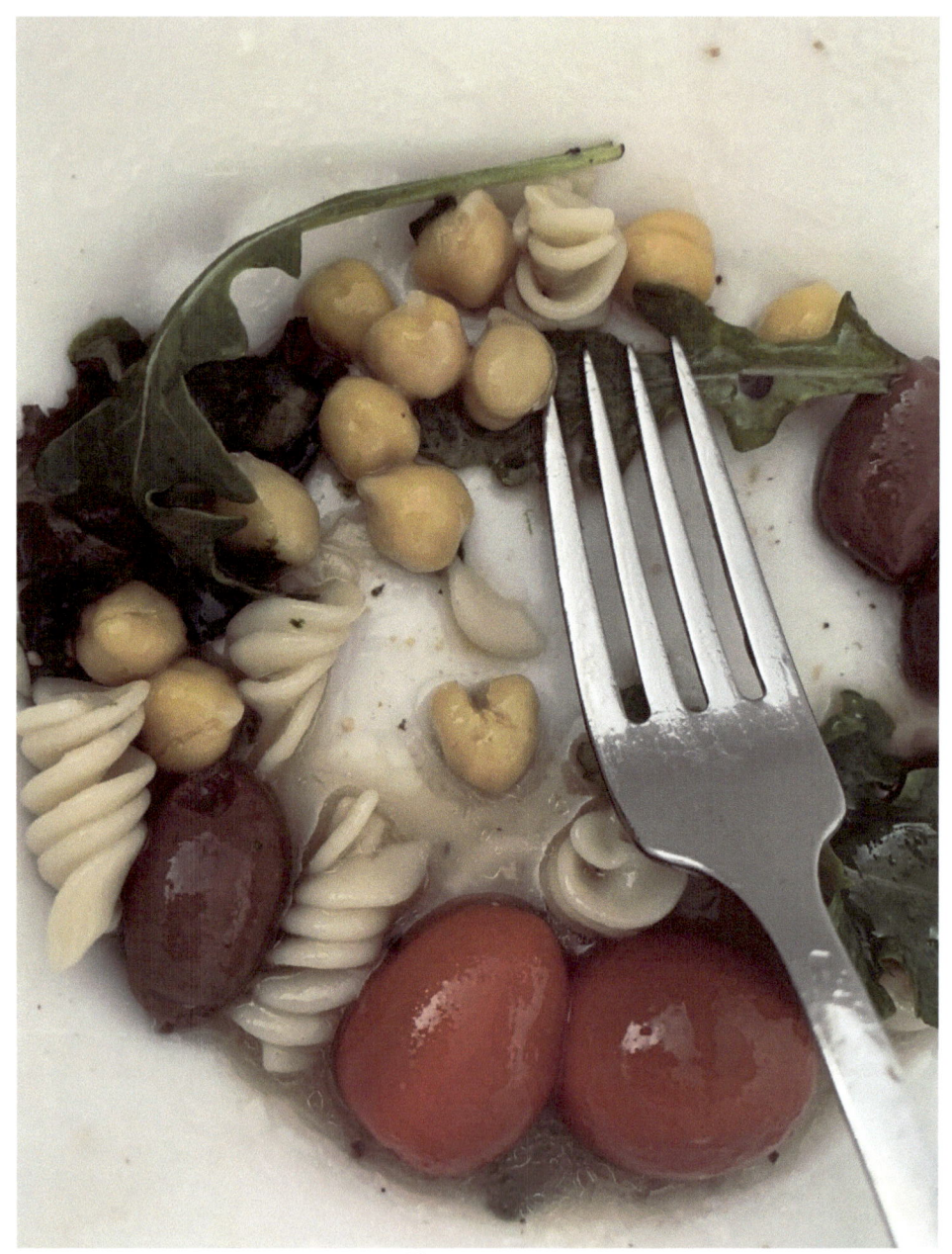

CHICKPEA

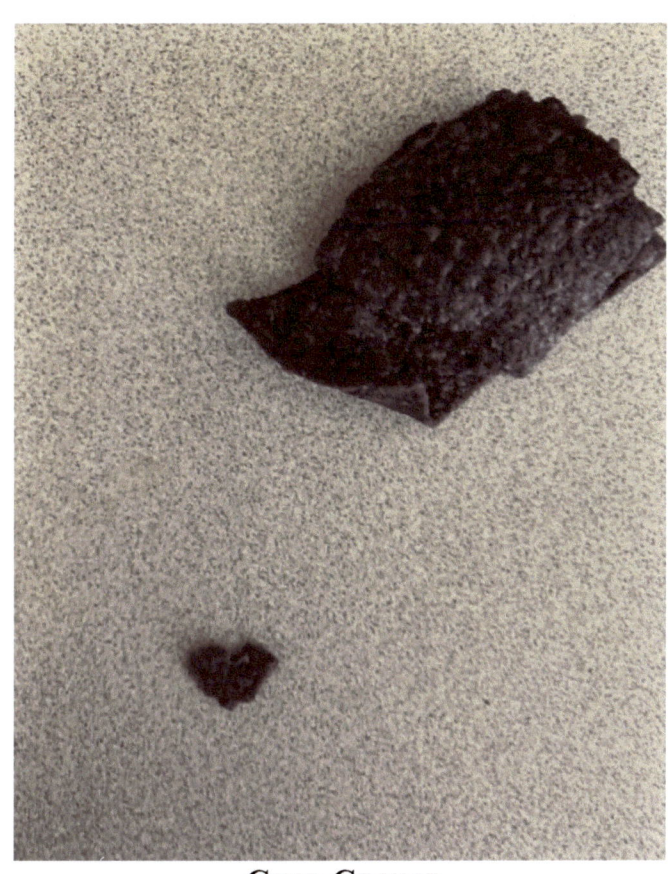

Chip Crumb

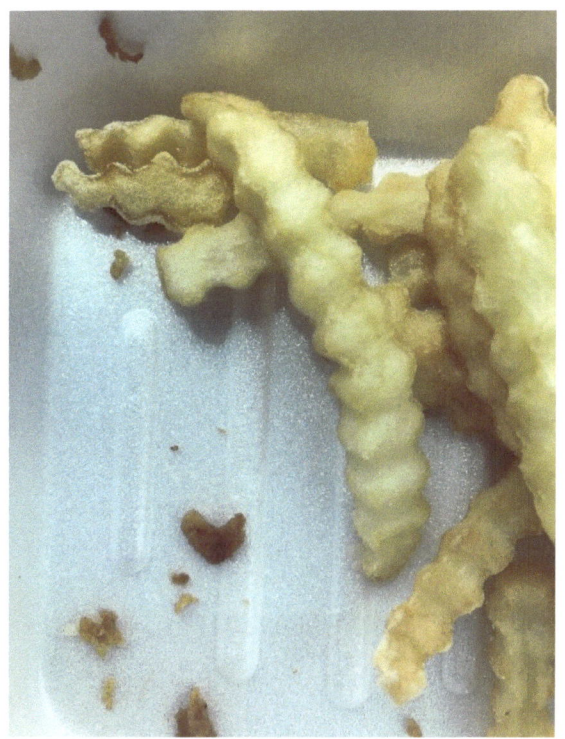

French Fry Crunchy

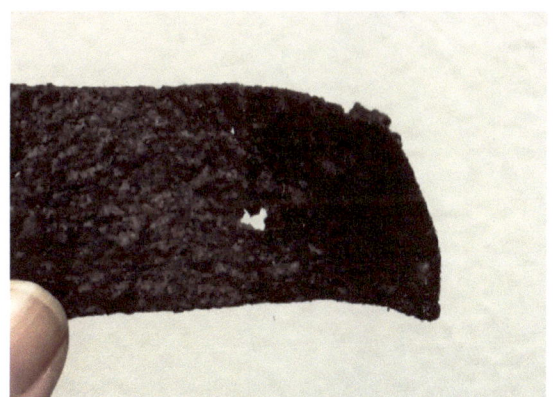

Blue Corn Chip

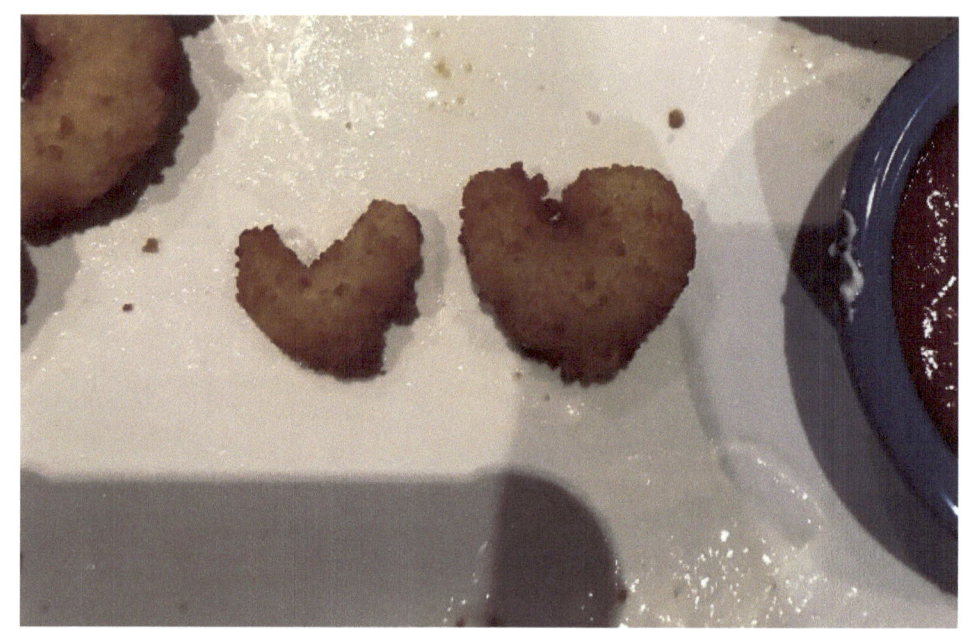
POPCORN SHRIMP

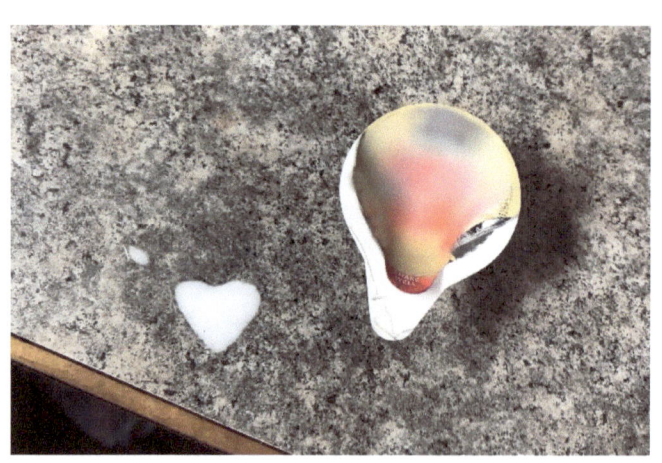
COFFEE CREAMER

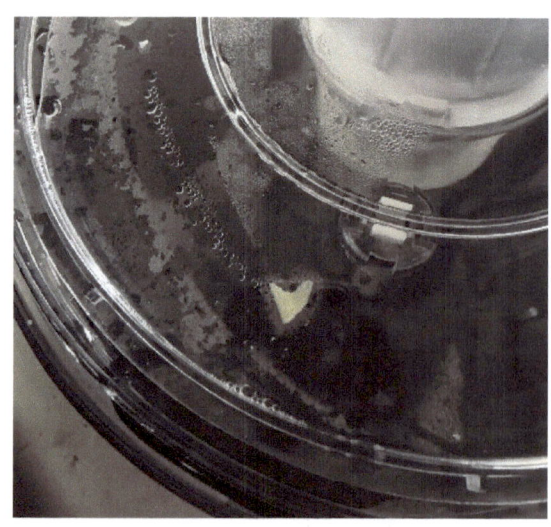
PIECE OF LIME

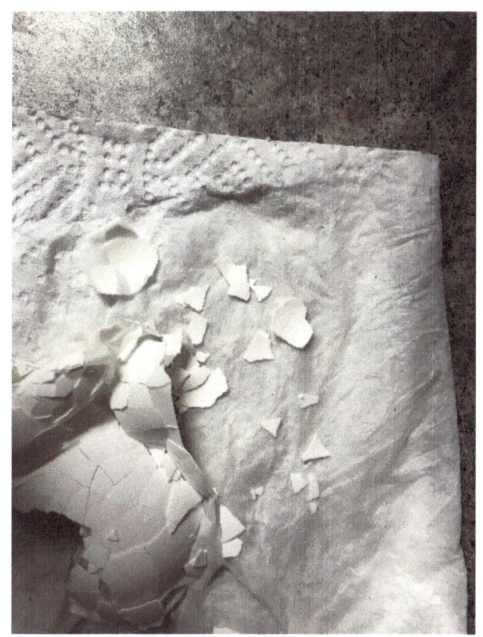
Hard Boiled Eggshell

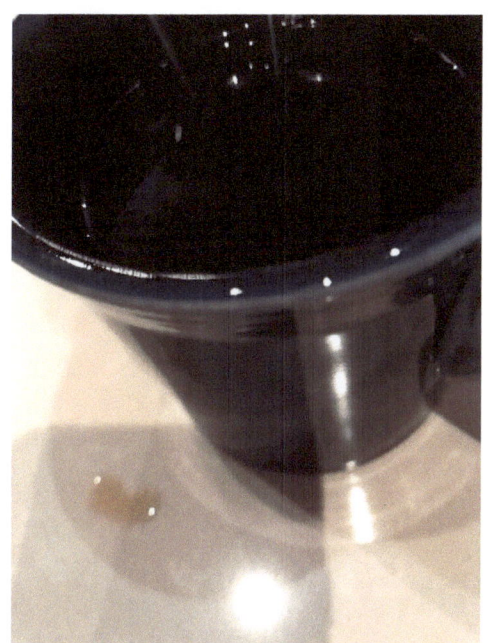
Coffee Spill

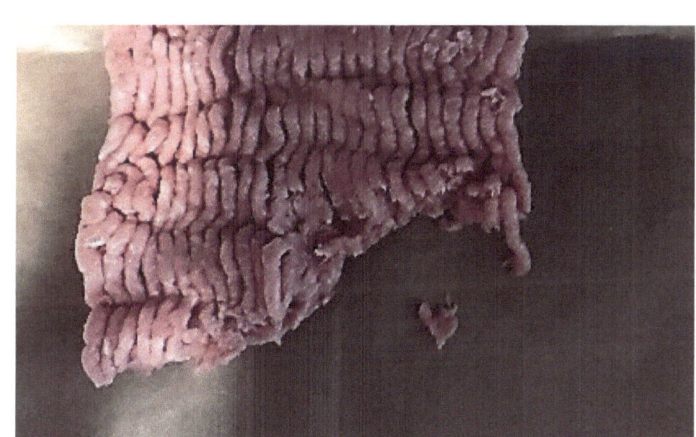
Ground Beef

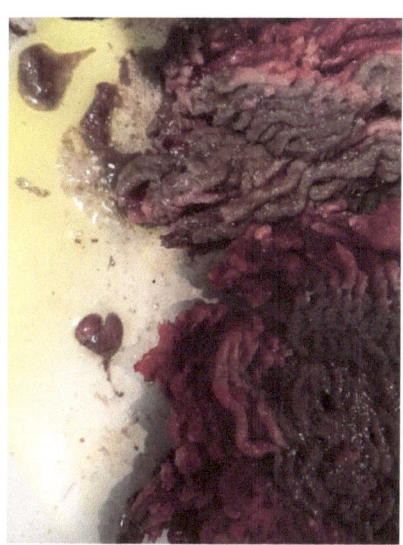
Hamburger Cooking

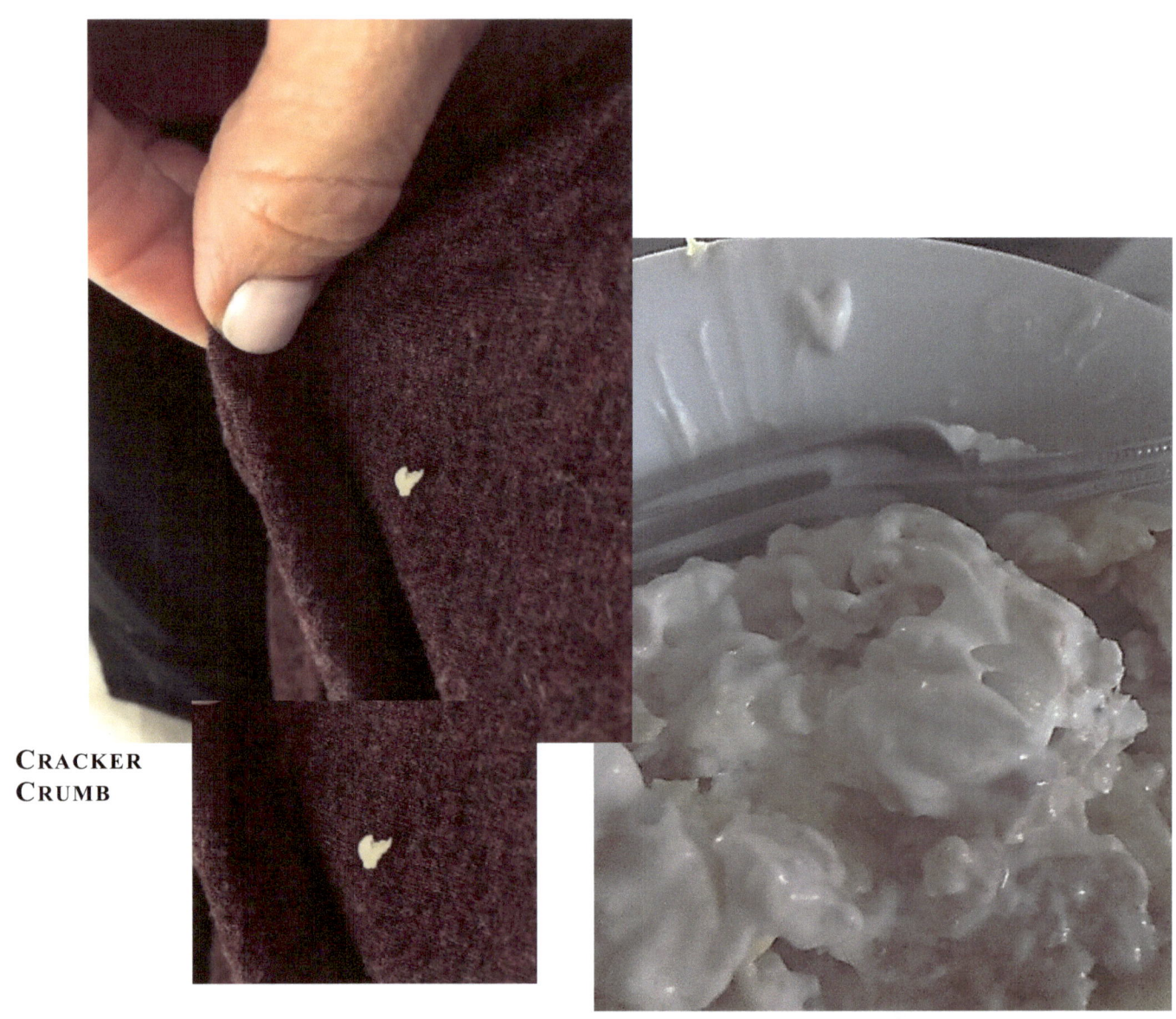

CRACKER CRUMB

SOUR CREAM

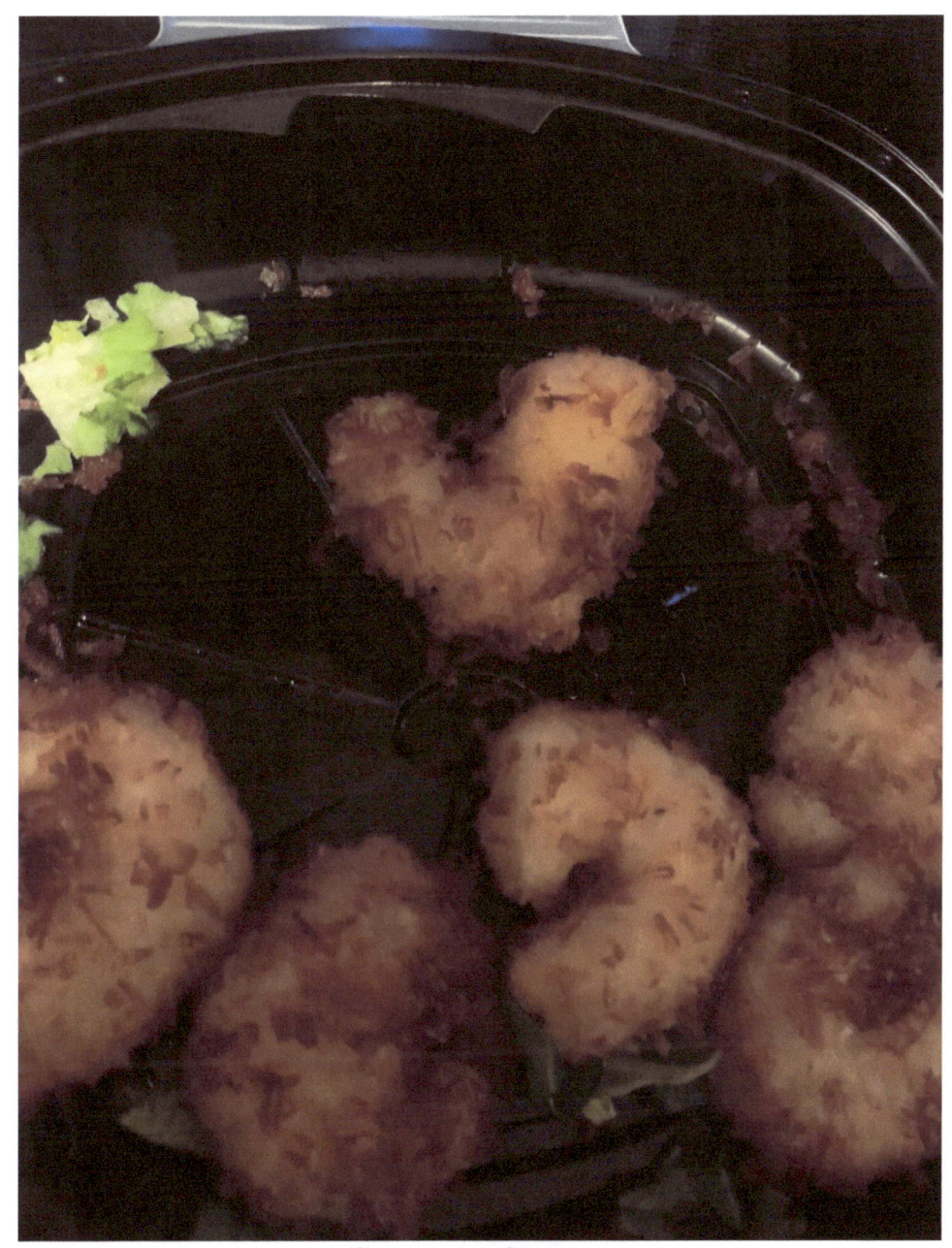

COCONUT SHRIMP

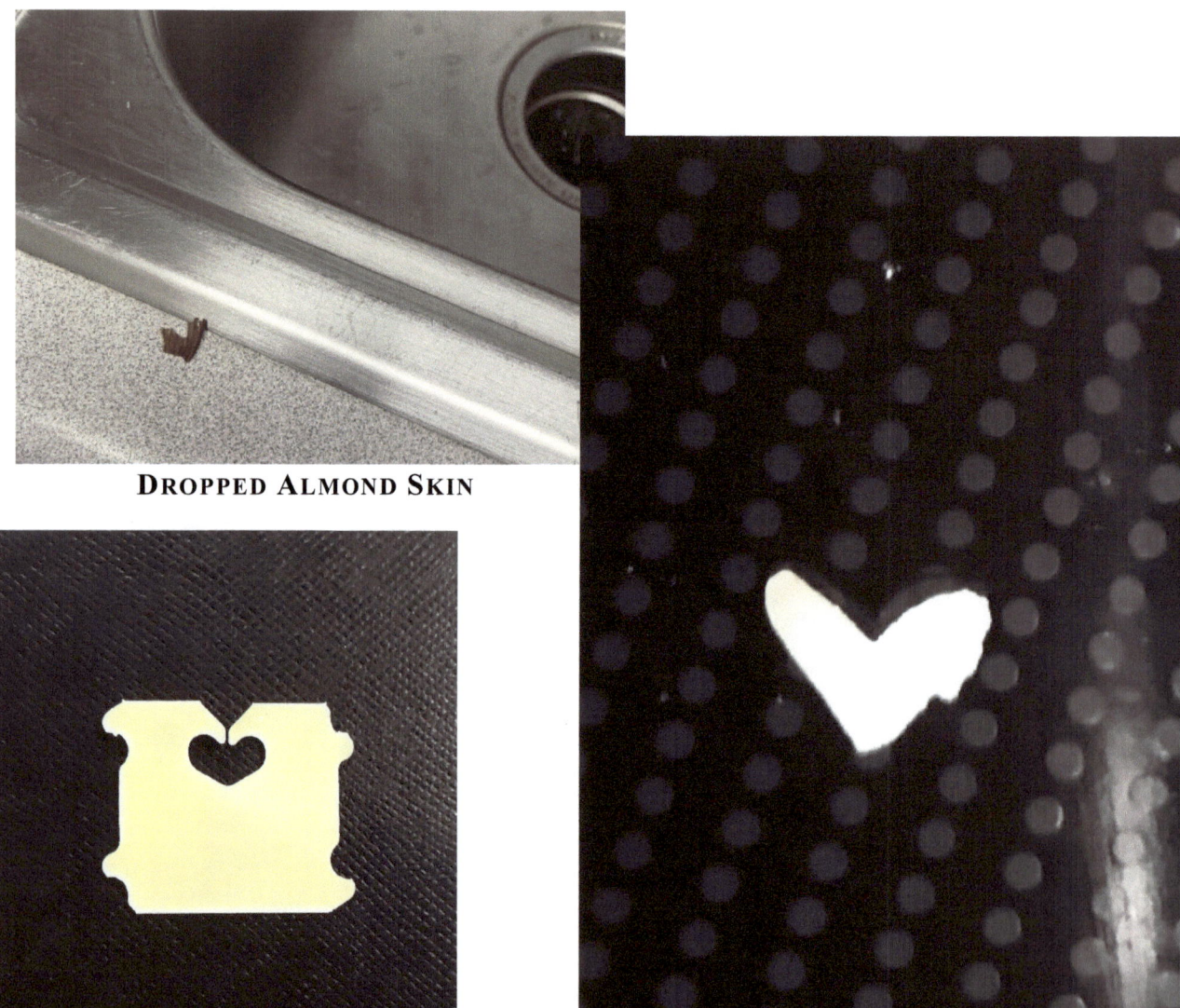

Dropped Almond Skin

Bread Tie

Rice on Stovetop

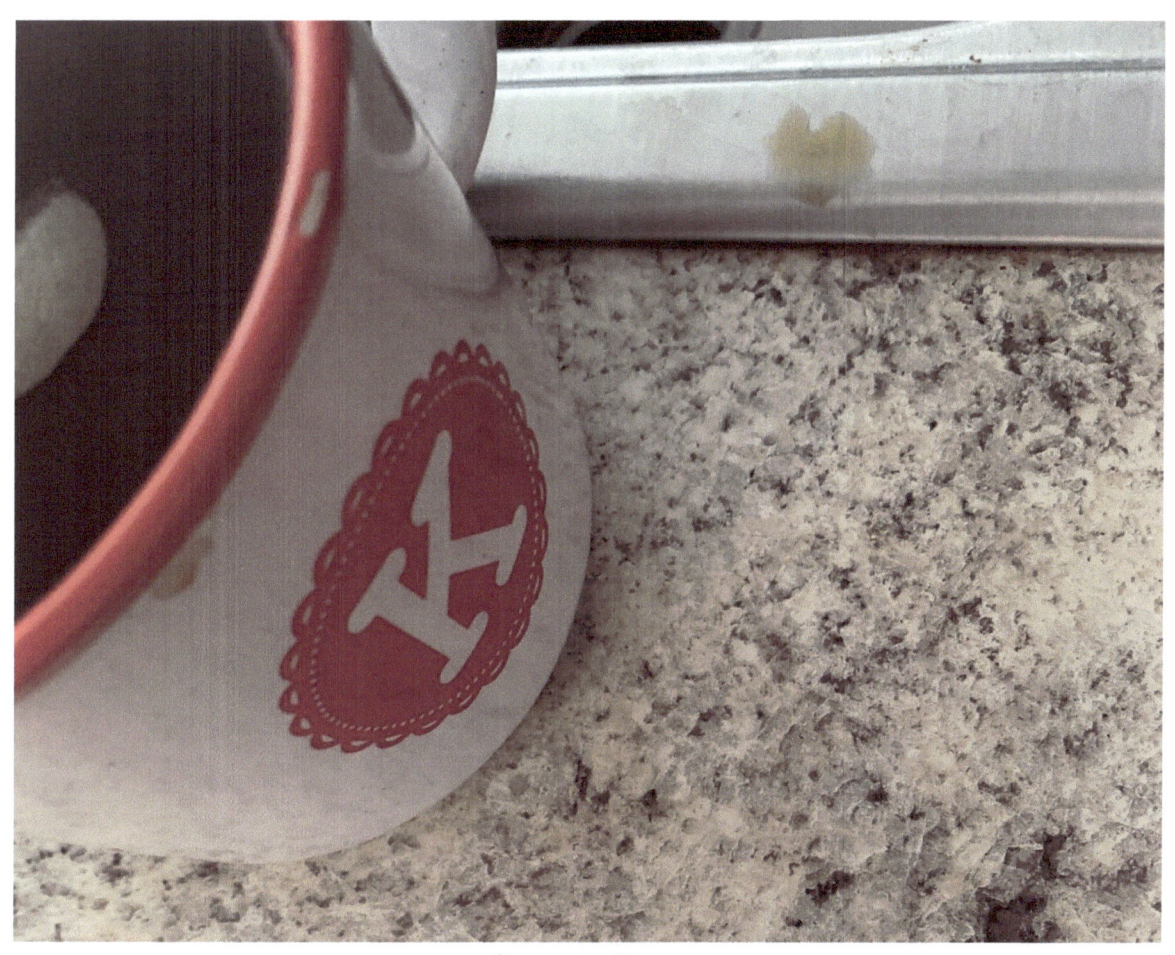

COFFEE DRIP

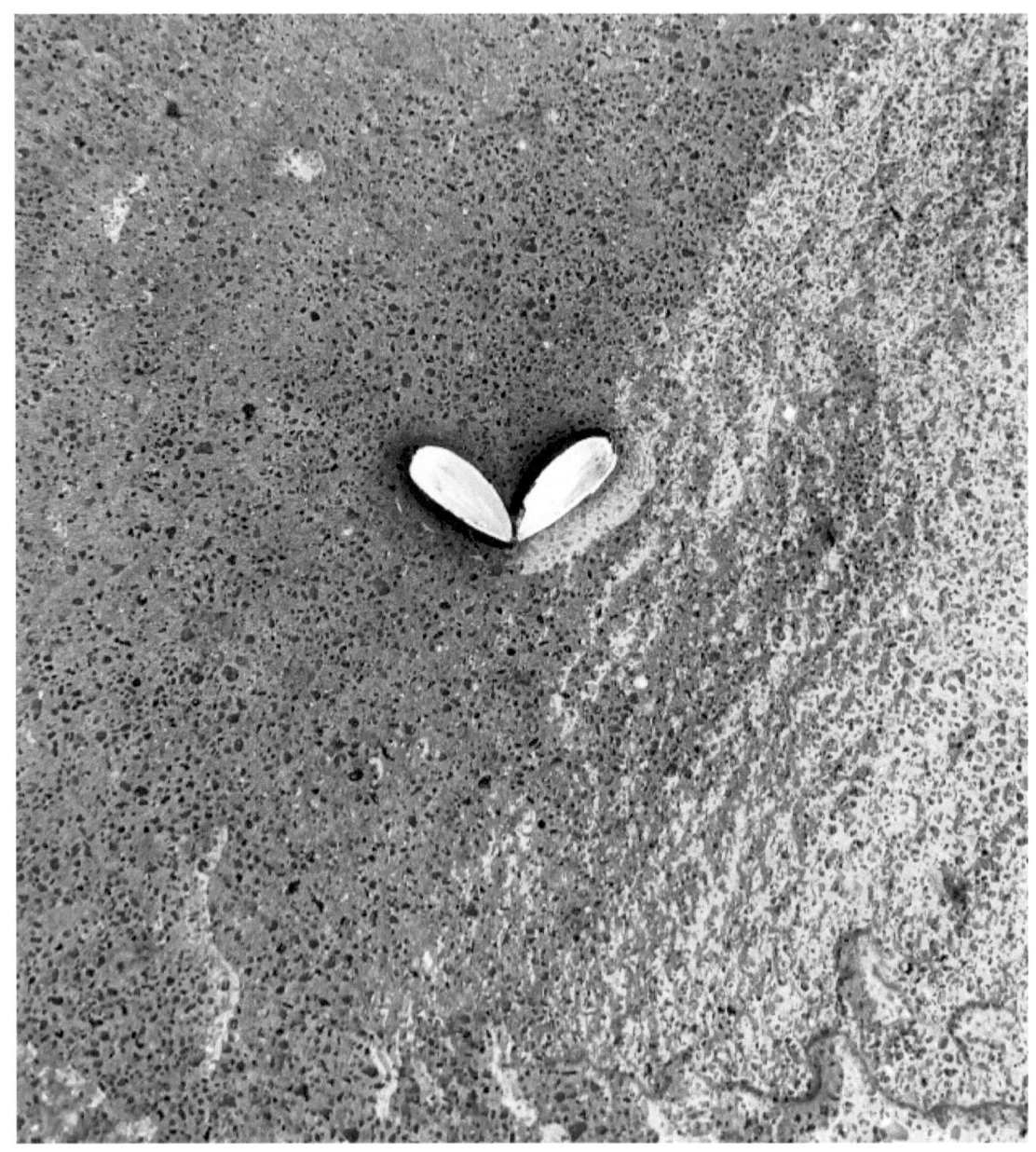

SUNFLOWER SEED

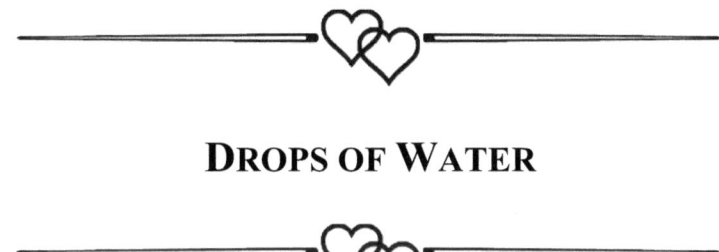

DROPS OF WATER

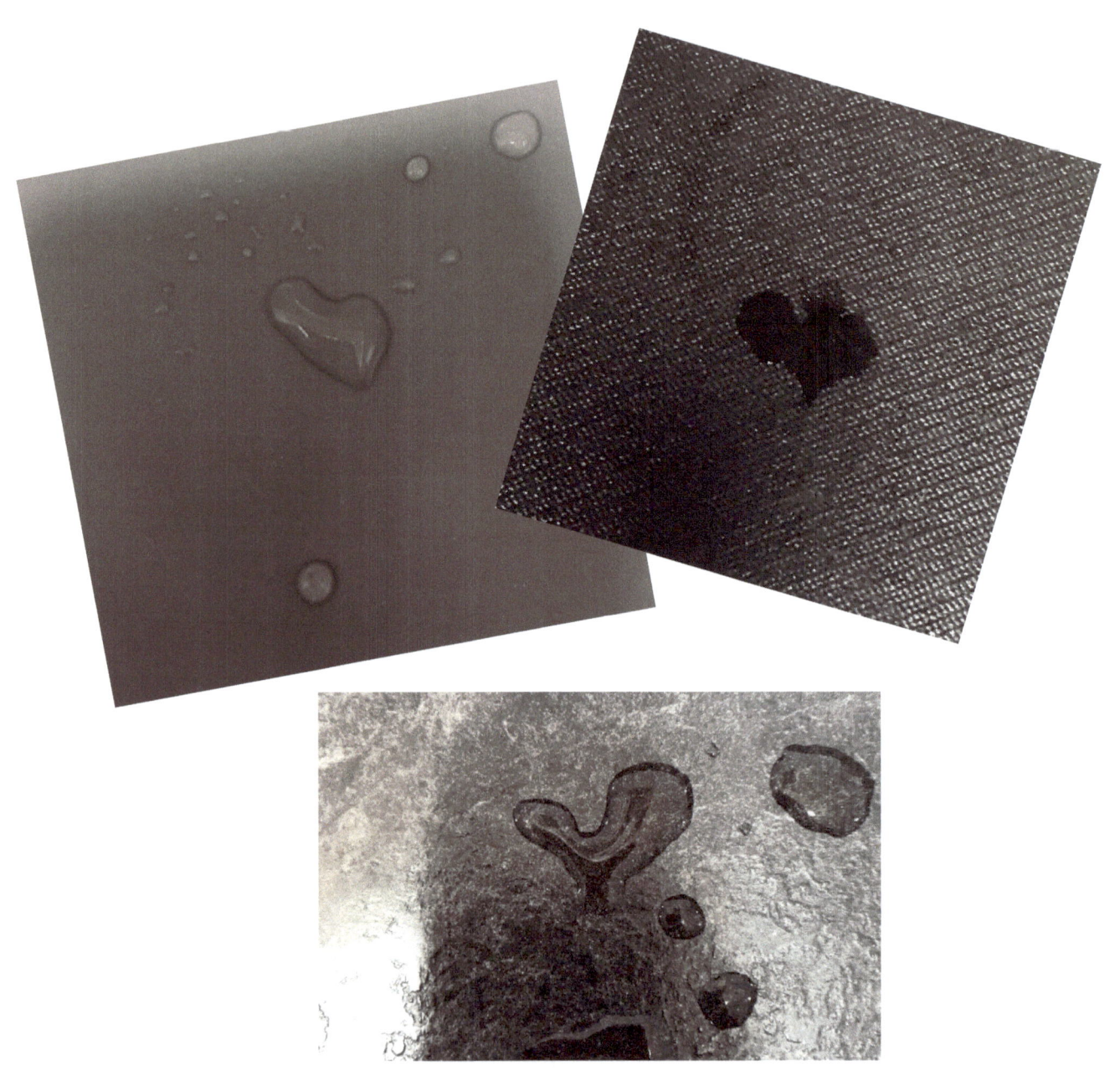

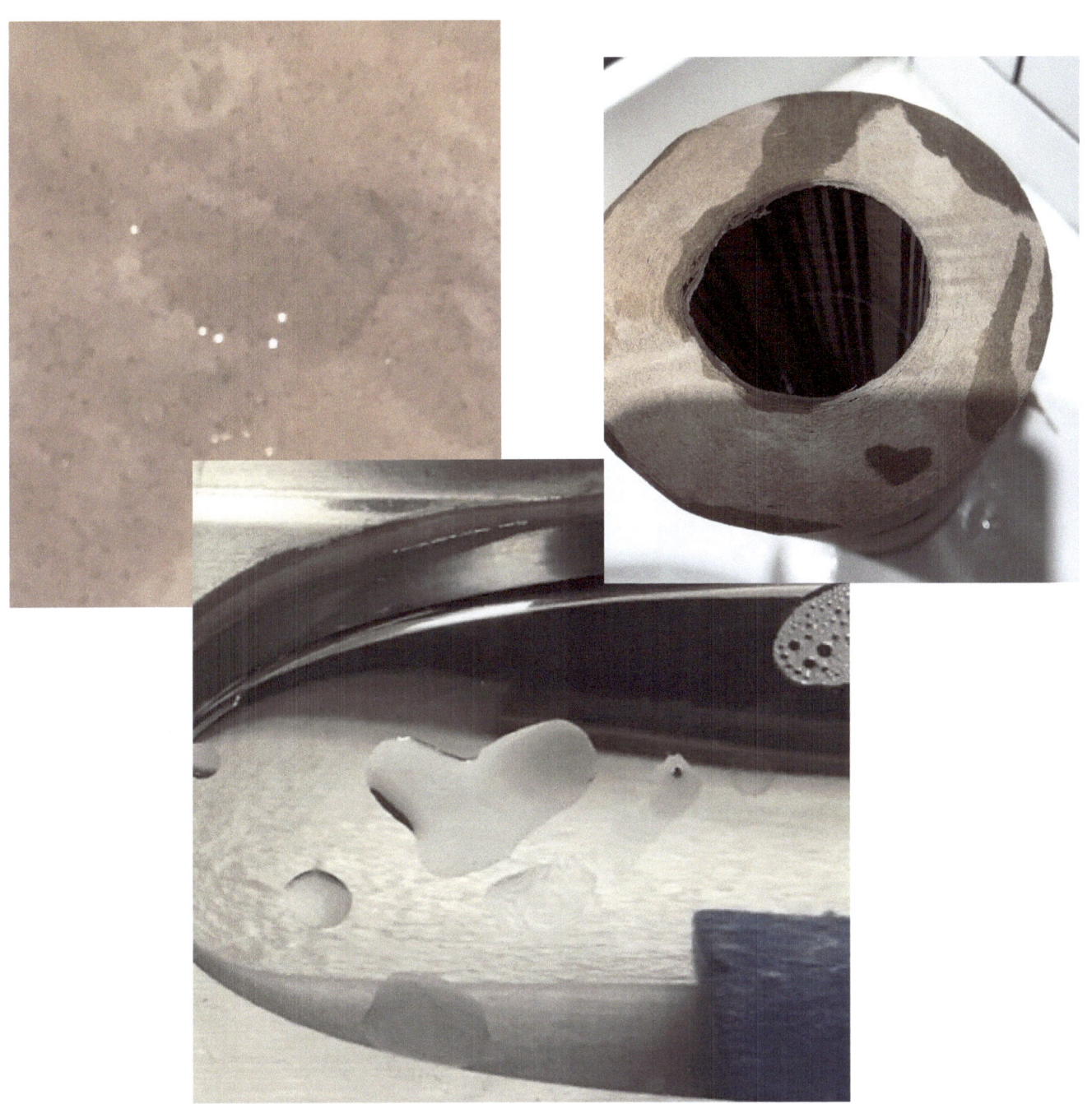

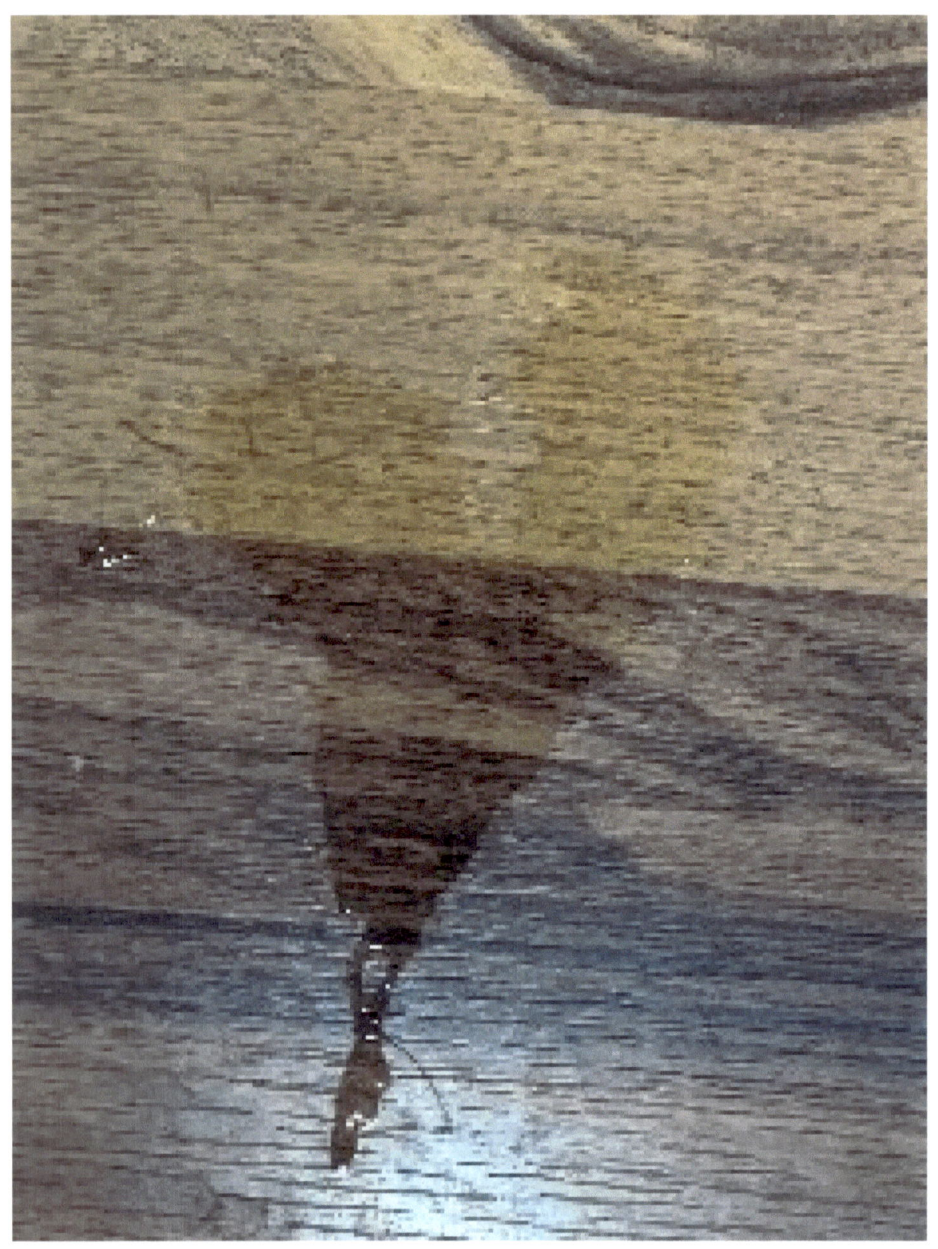

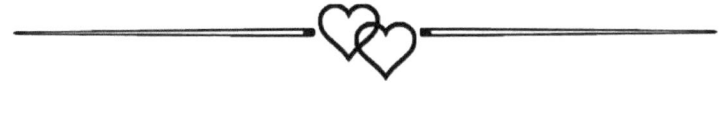

Miscellaneous

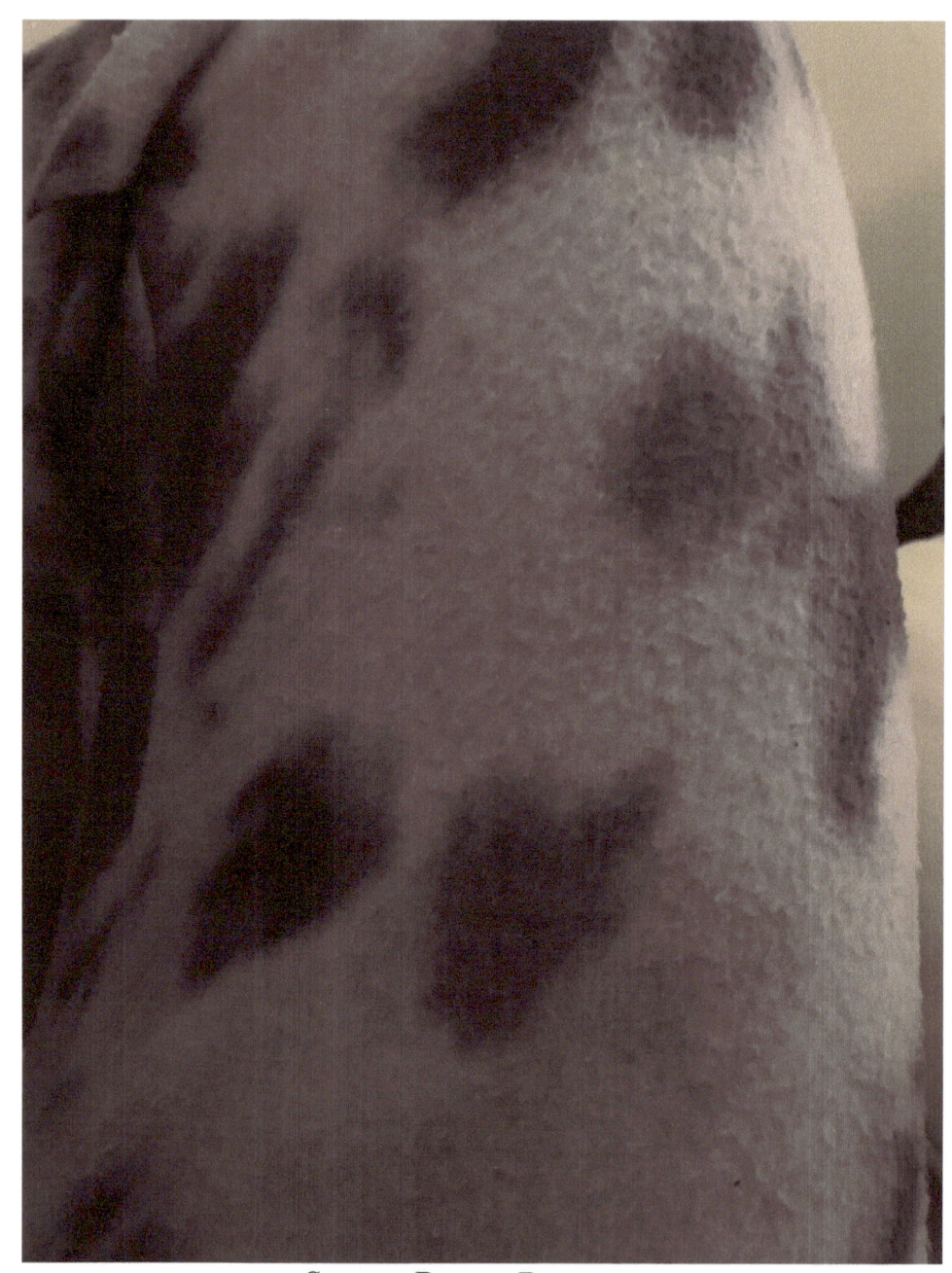

SWEAT PANTS PATTERN

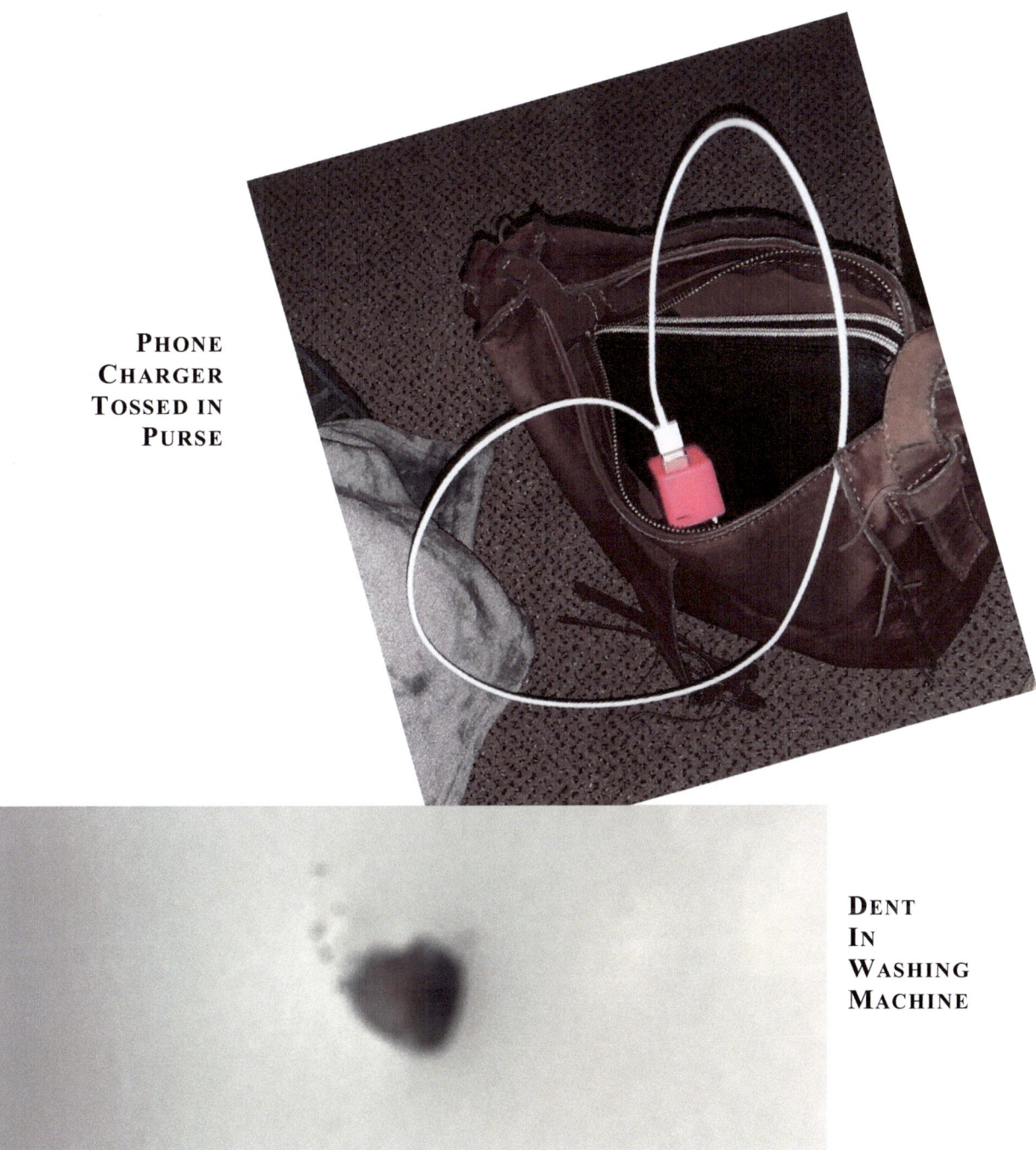

Phone Charger Tossed in Purse

Dent In Washing Machine

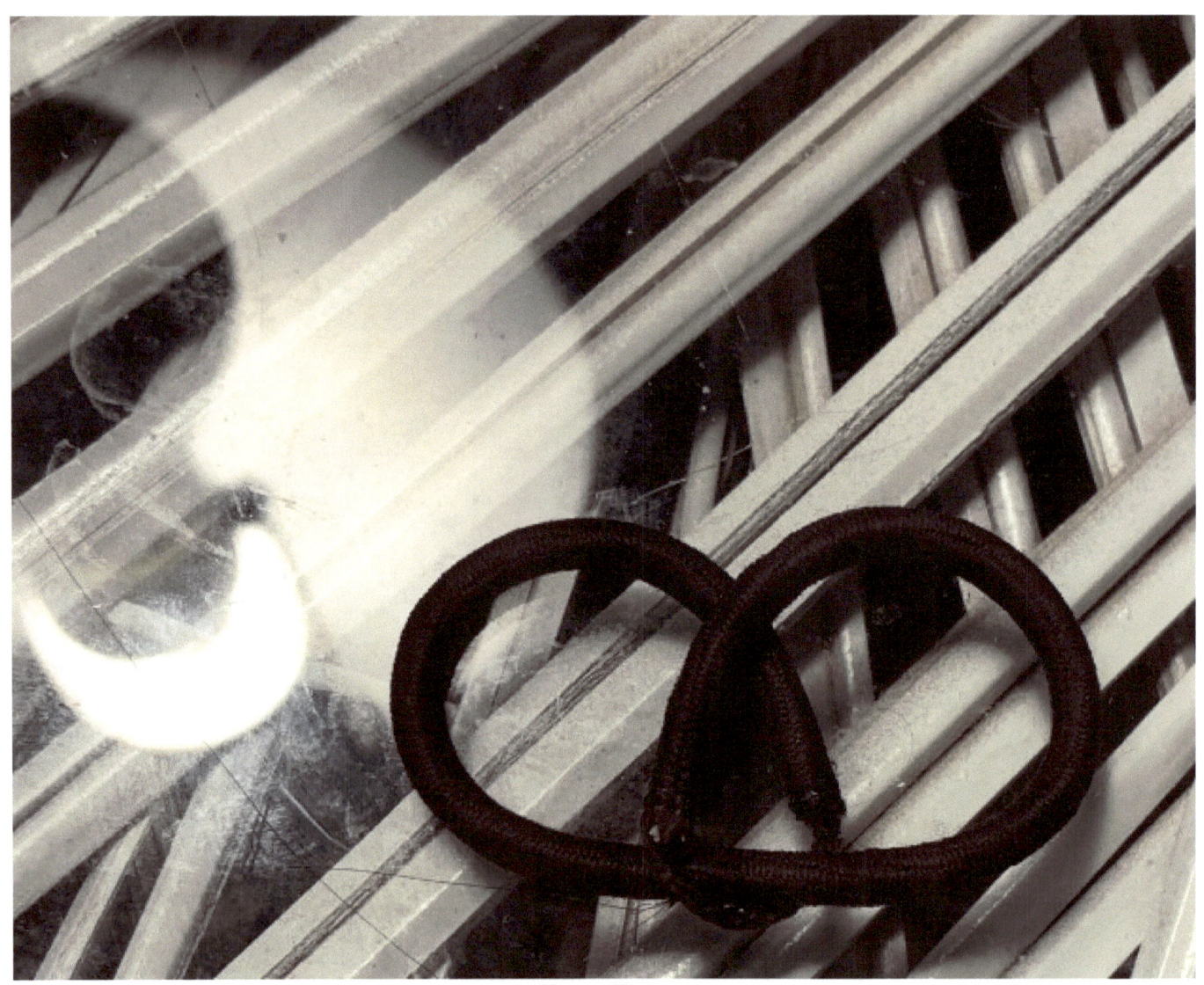
HAIR TIE

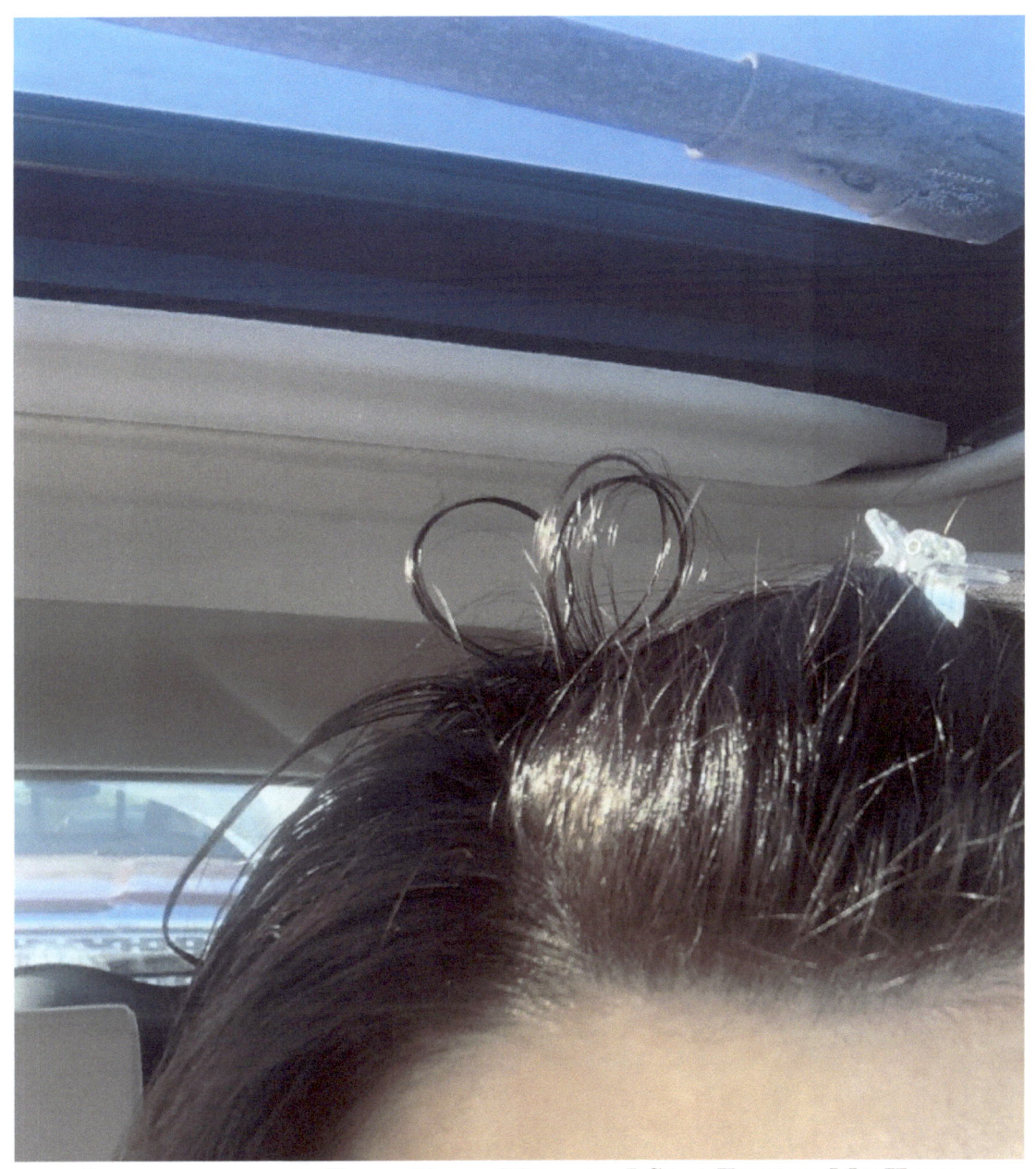

LOOKING IN THE REAR VIEW MIRROR I SAW THIS IN MY HAIR

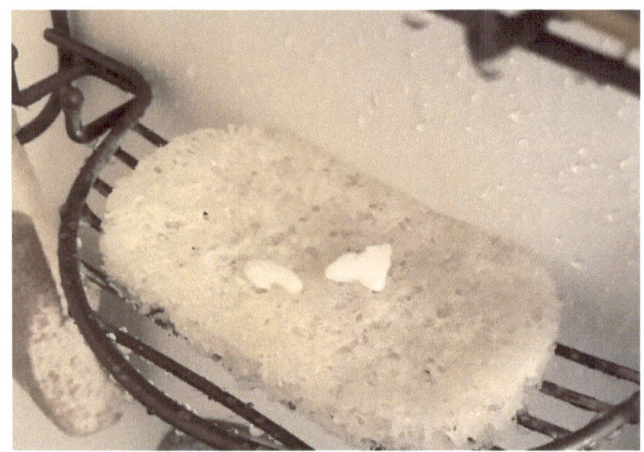

Soap Pieces

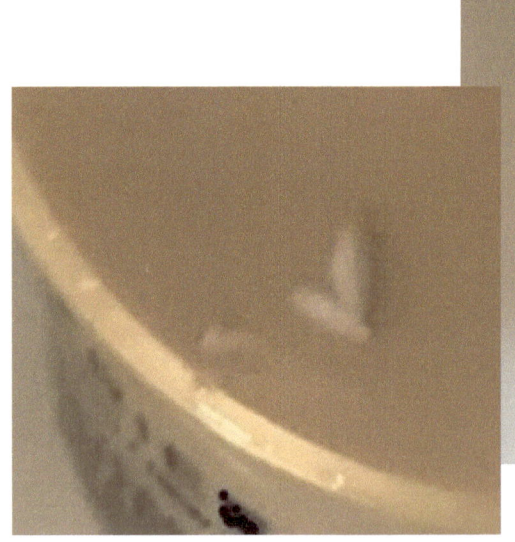

Hair Conditioner Drop

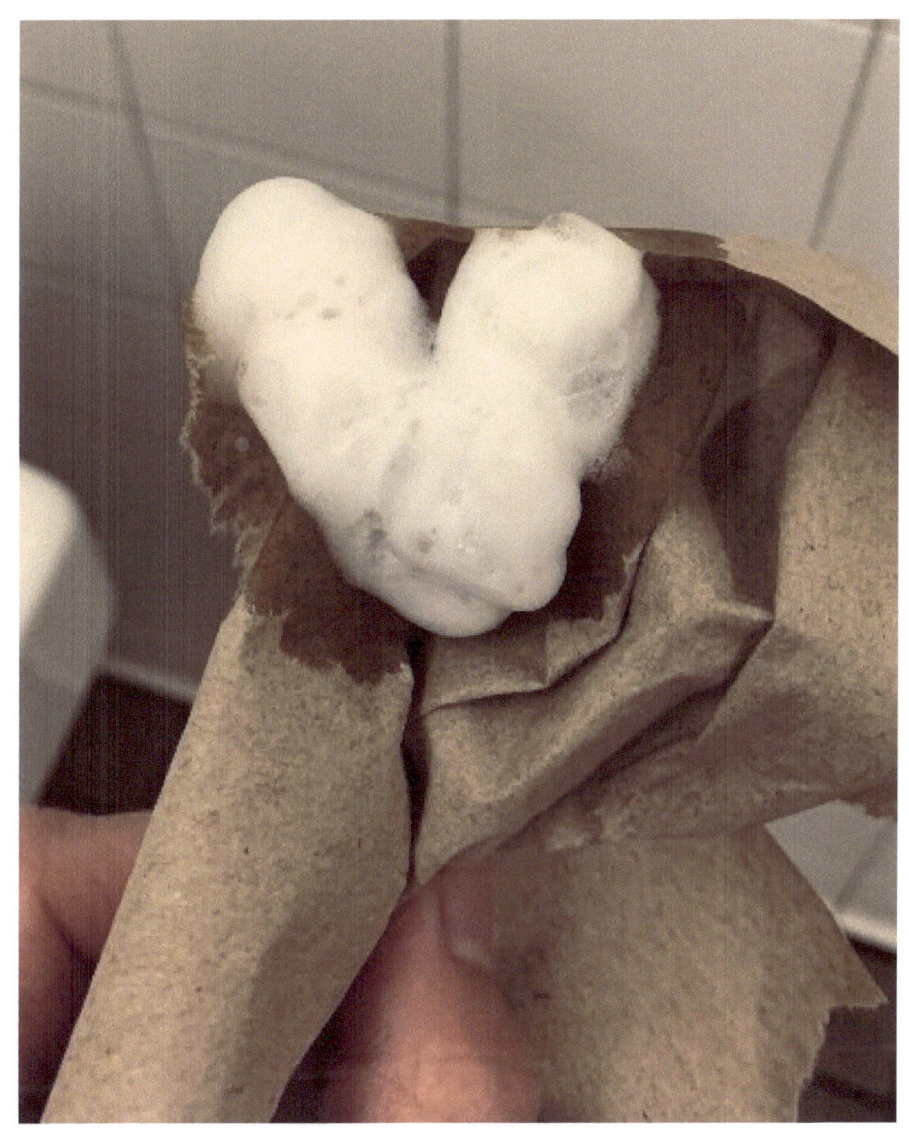

SOAP FROM AIRPORT DISPENSER

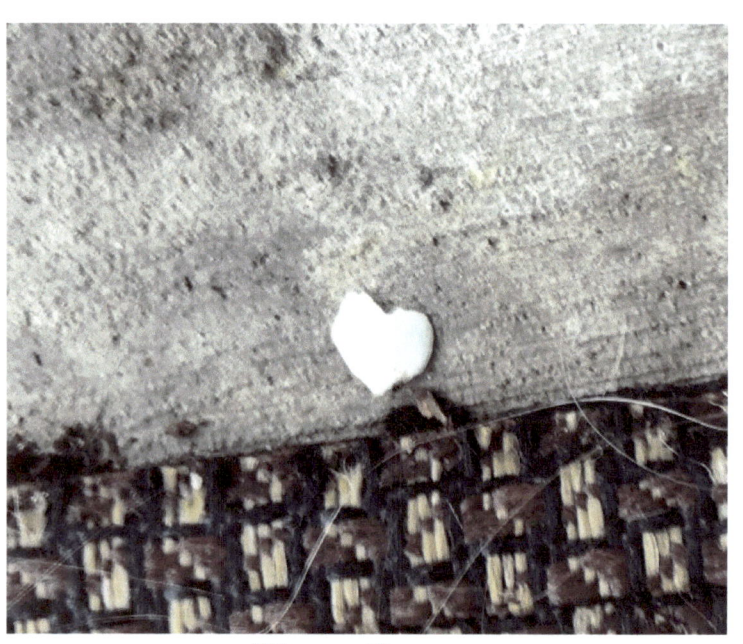

White Rock

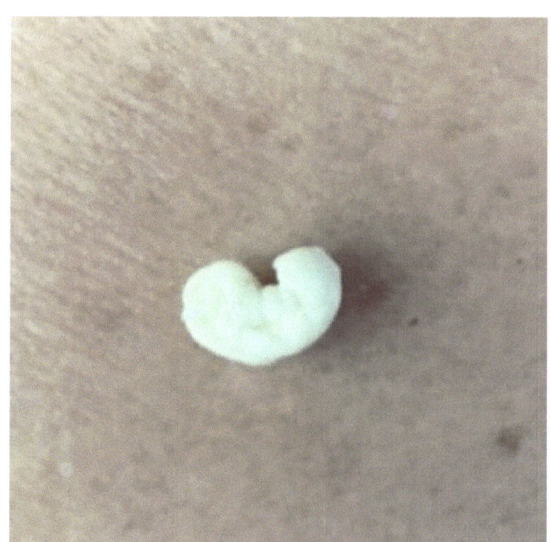

Rolled Up Gum

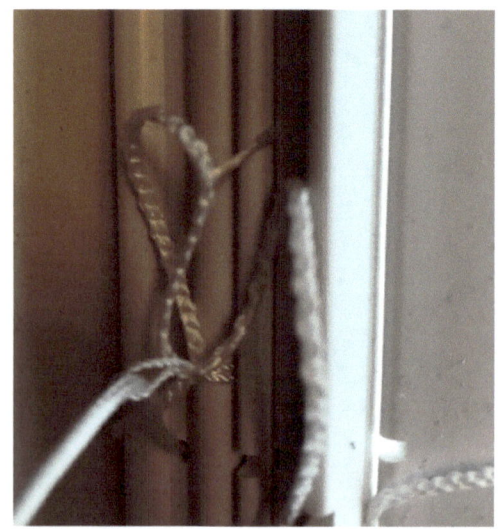

Mini Blind String

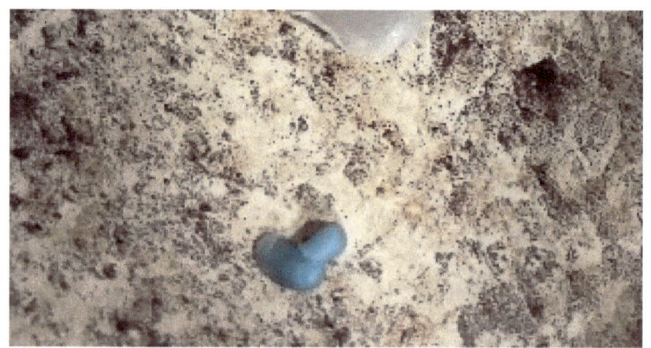

Candle Wax

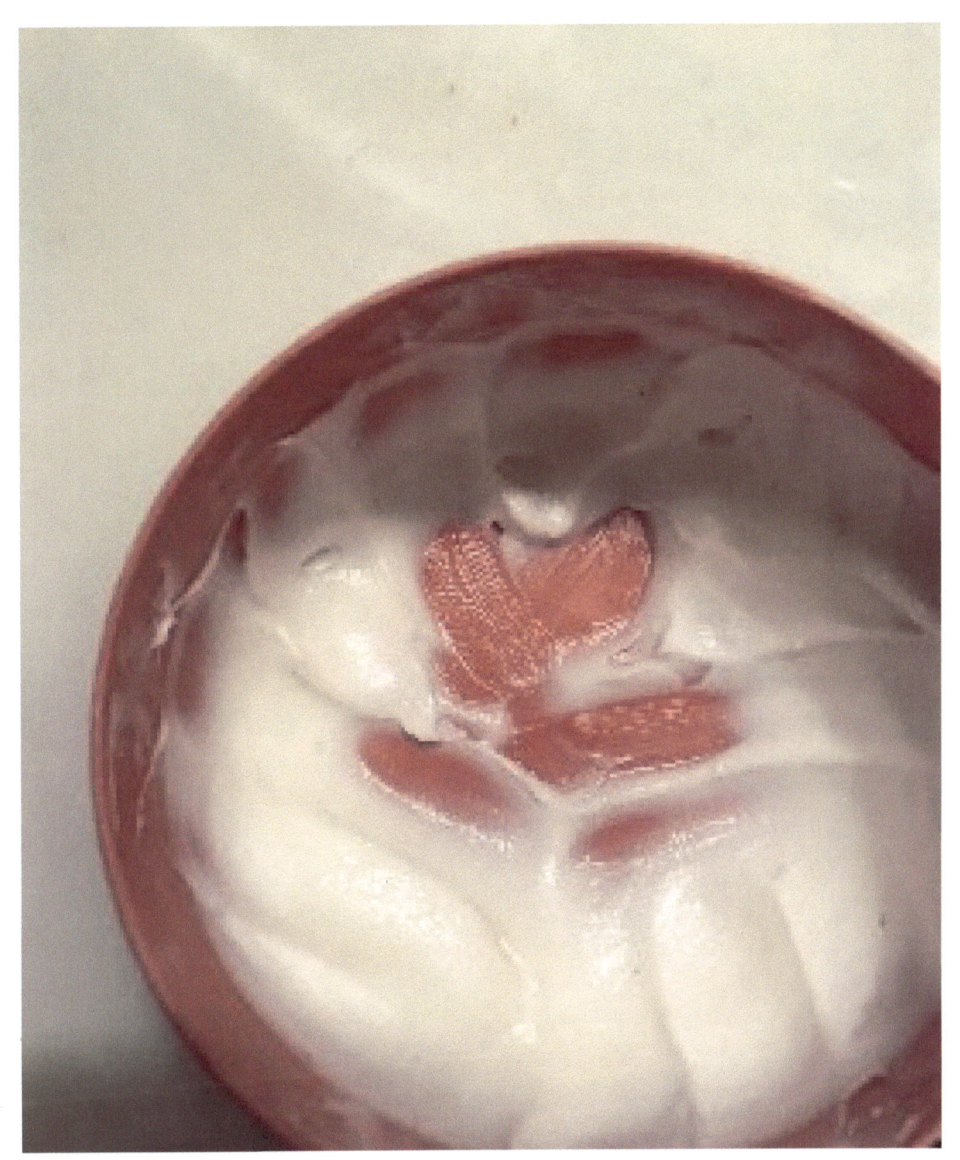

LOTION SWIPE

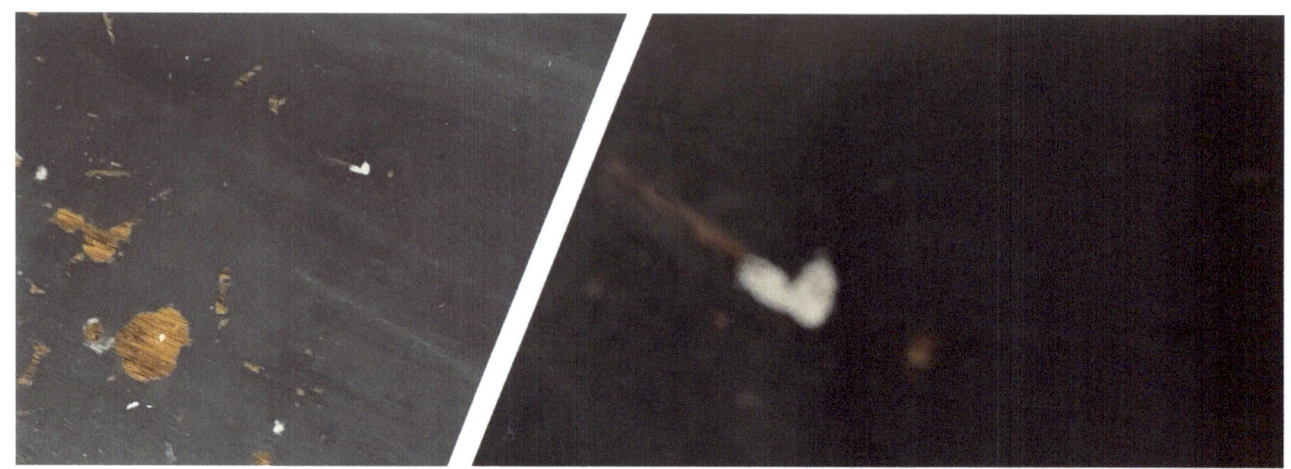

DESK SCRAPES, FAR AWAY AND CLOSE UP

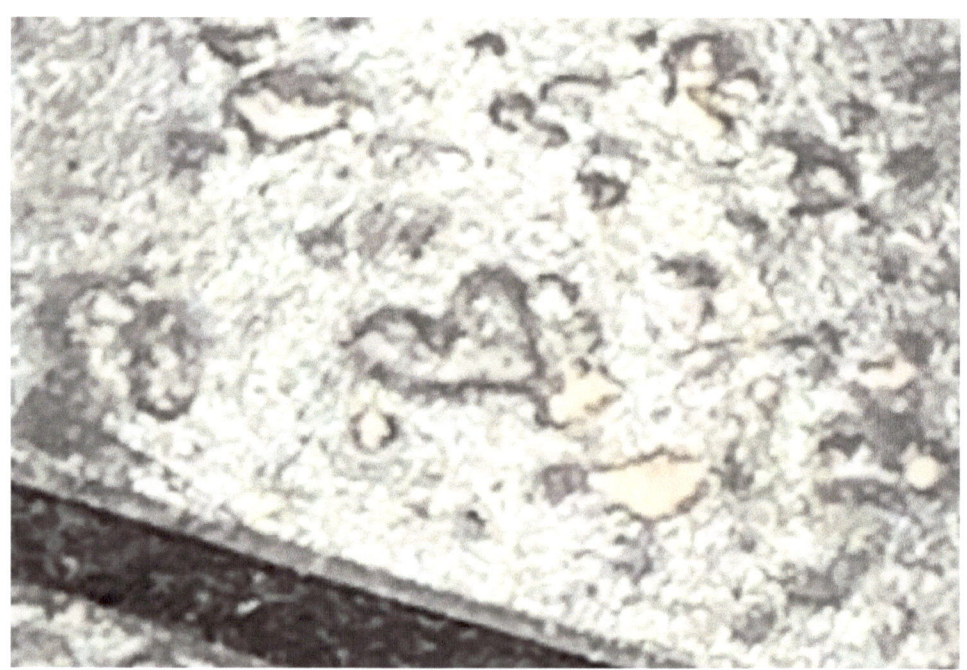

AIRPORT FLOOR PATTERN

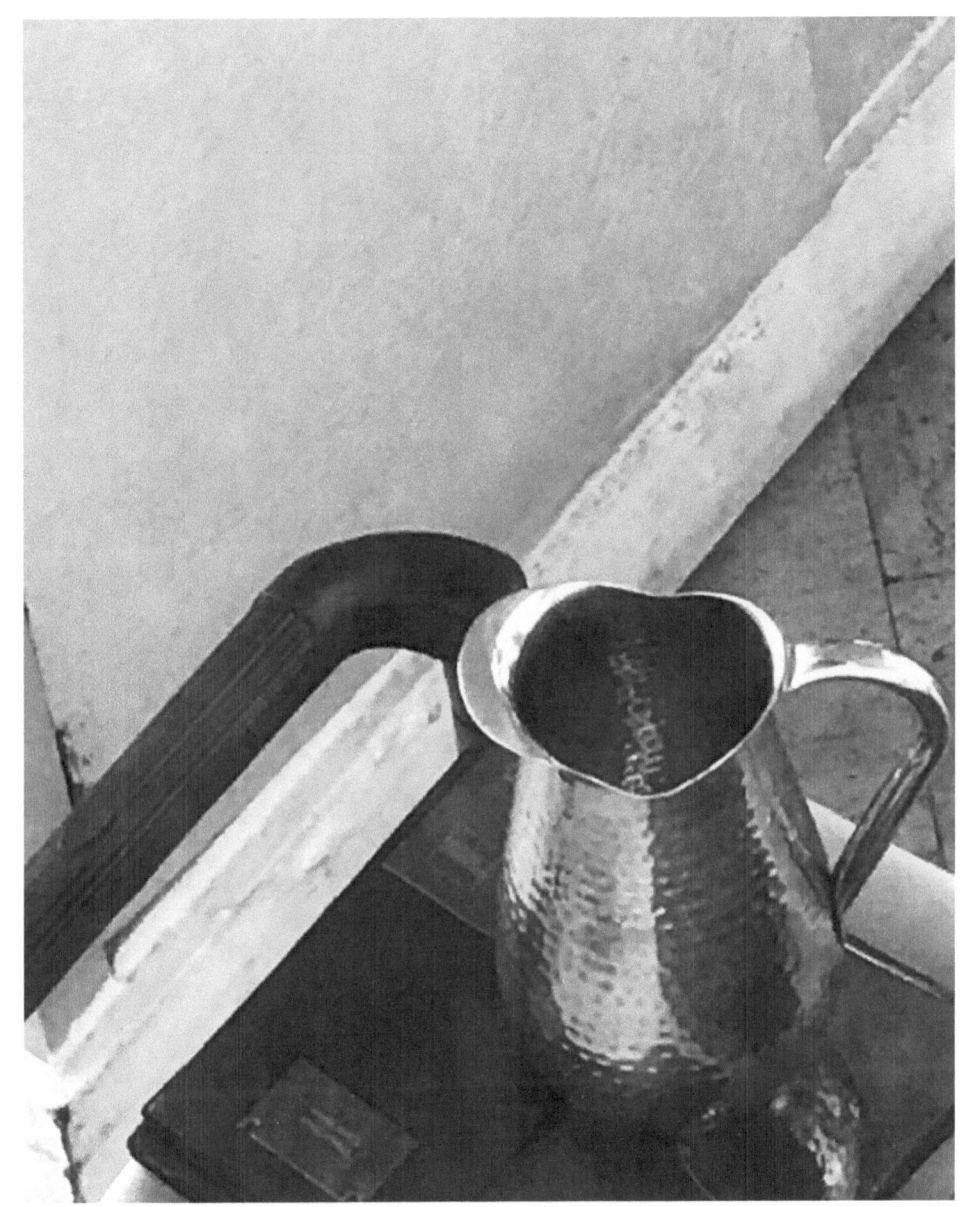

RESTAURANT PITCHER

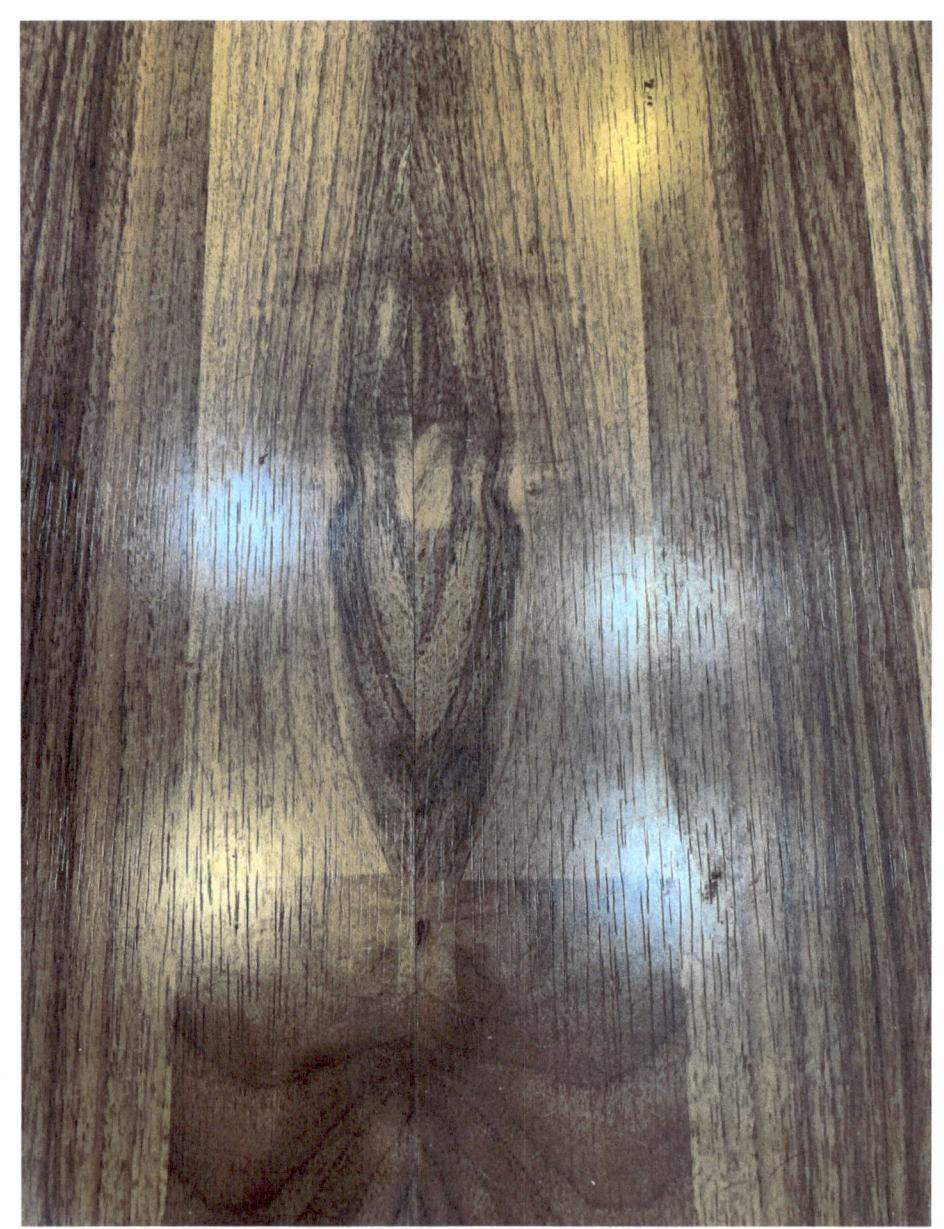

GRAIN IN HARDWOOD FLOOR

PAPER

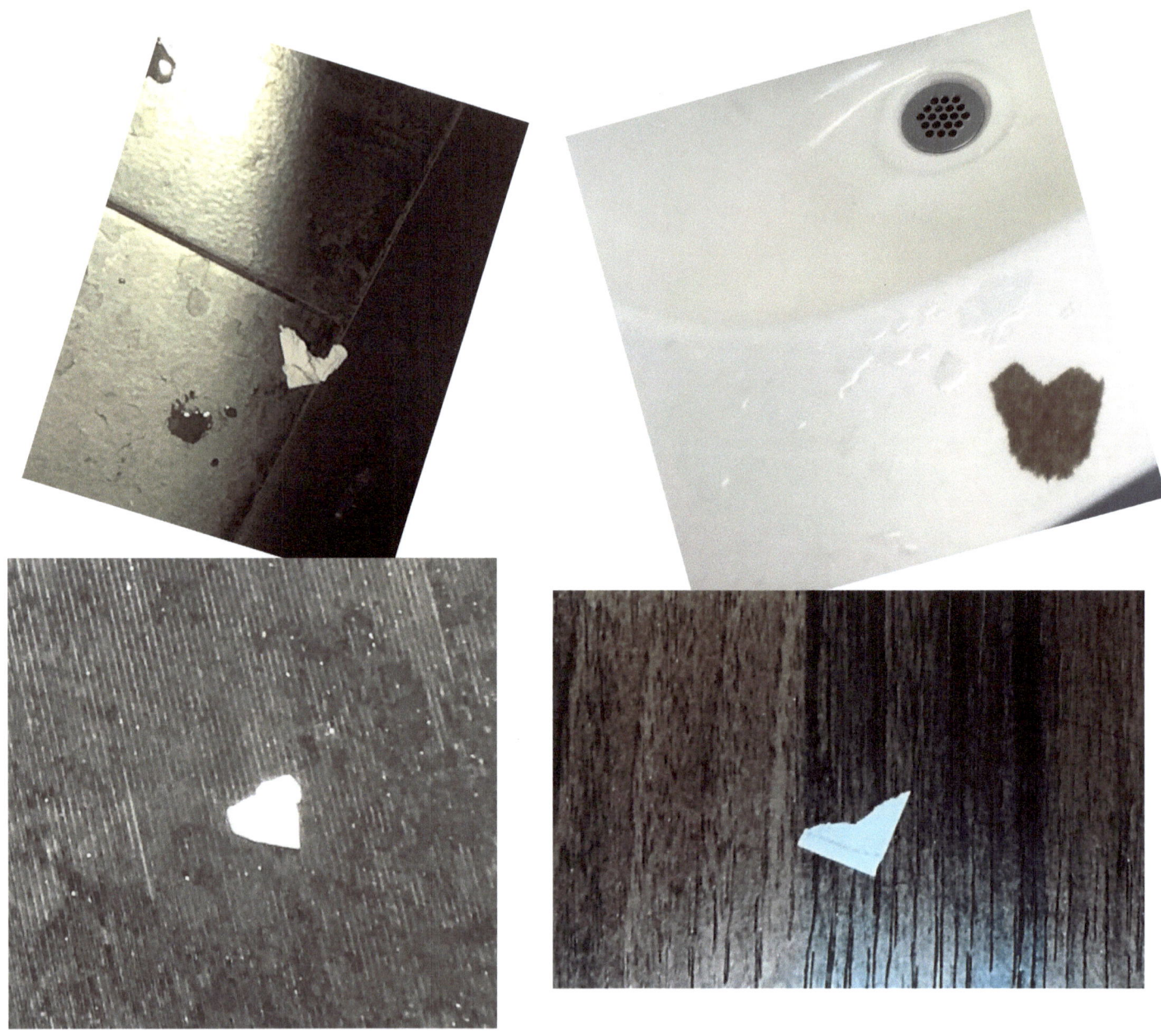

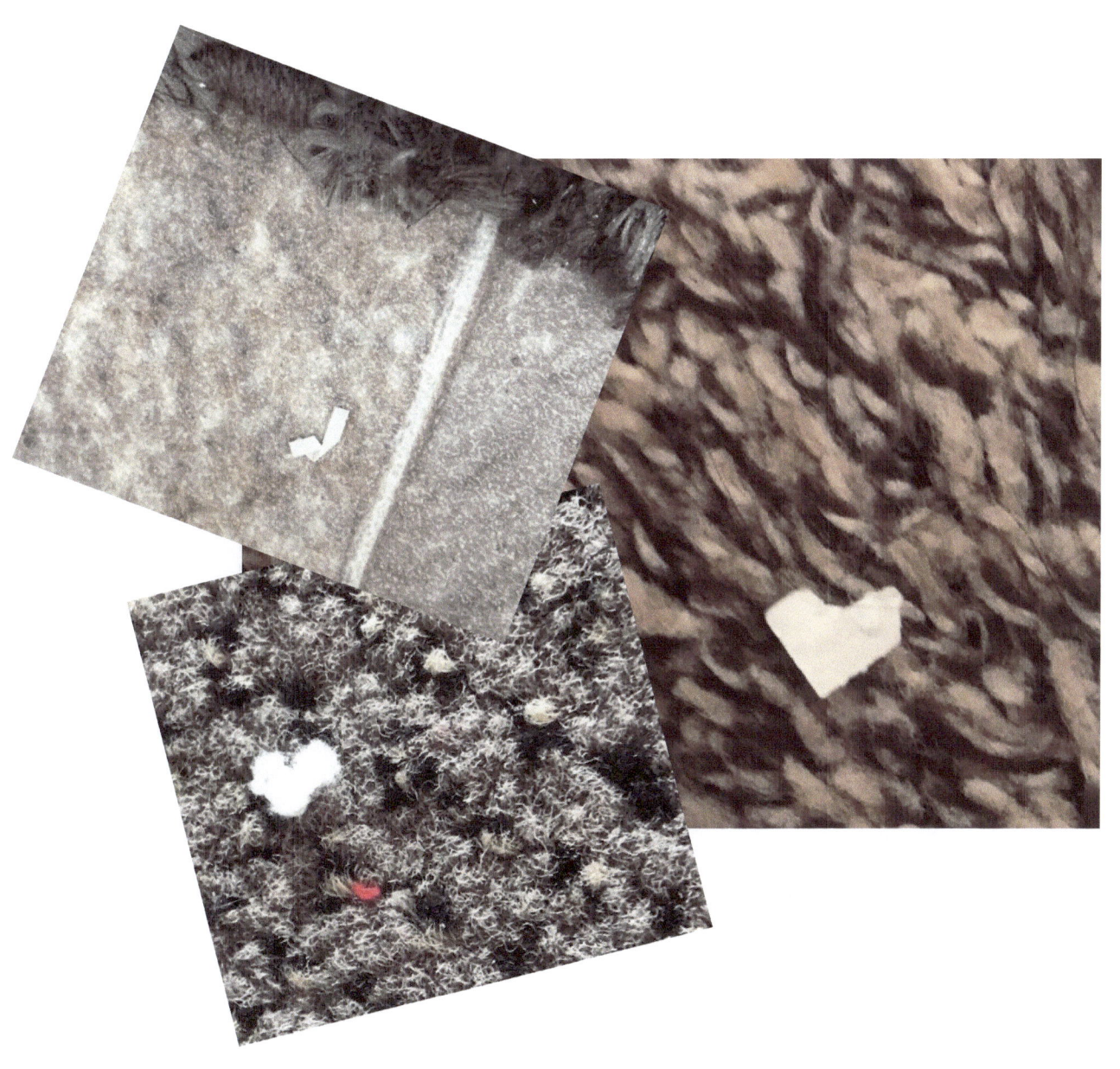

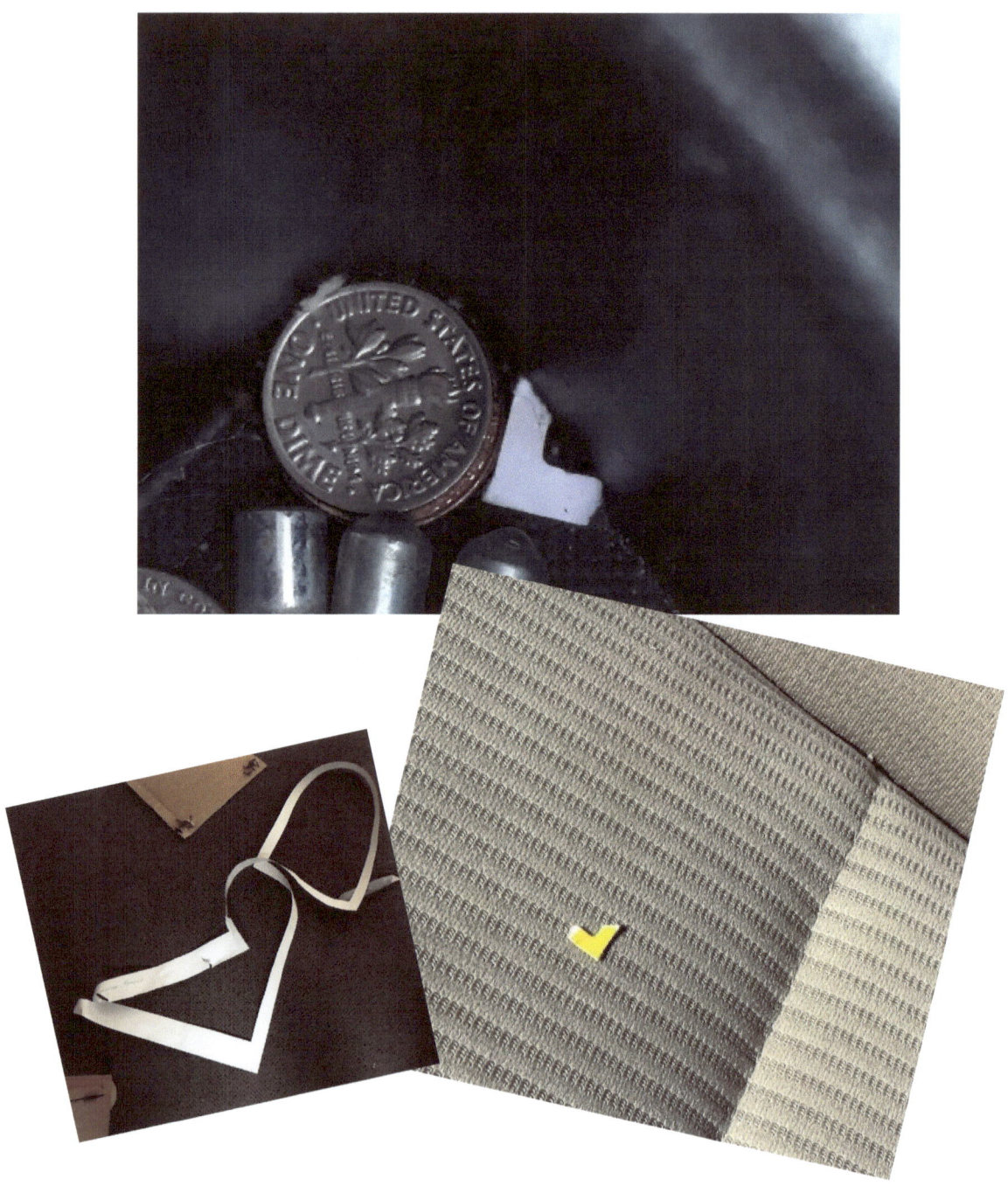

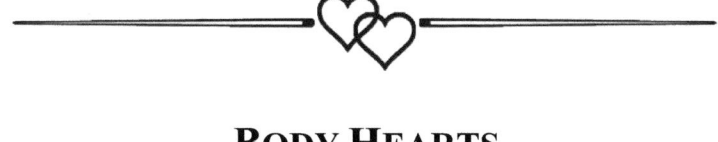

BODY HEARTS

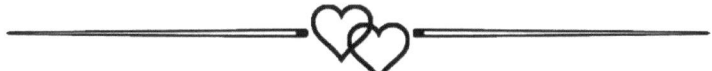

Will's Toe

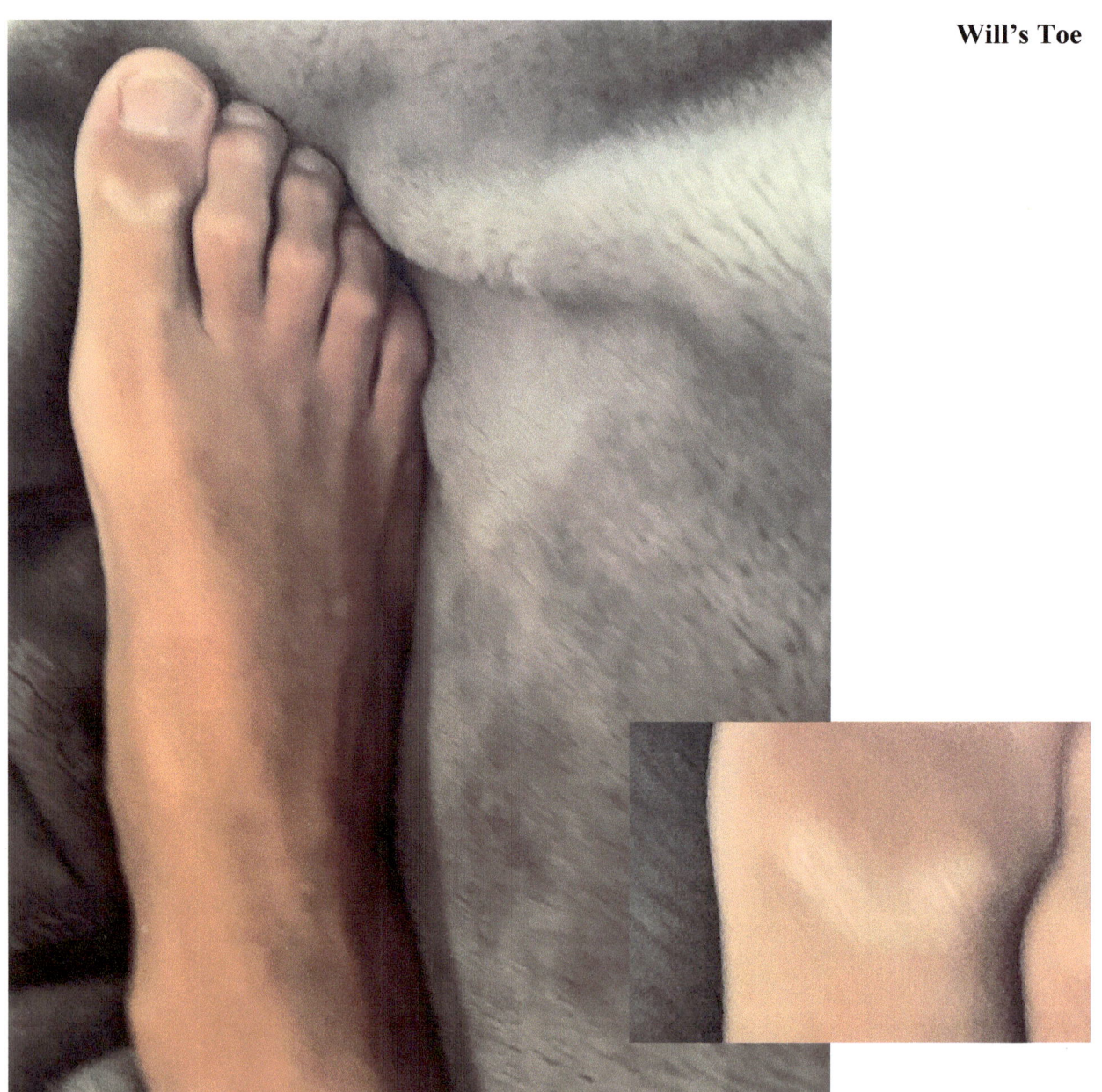

Kim's Arm

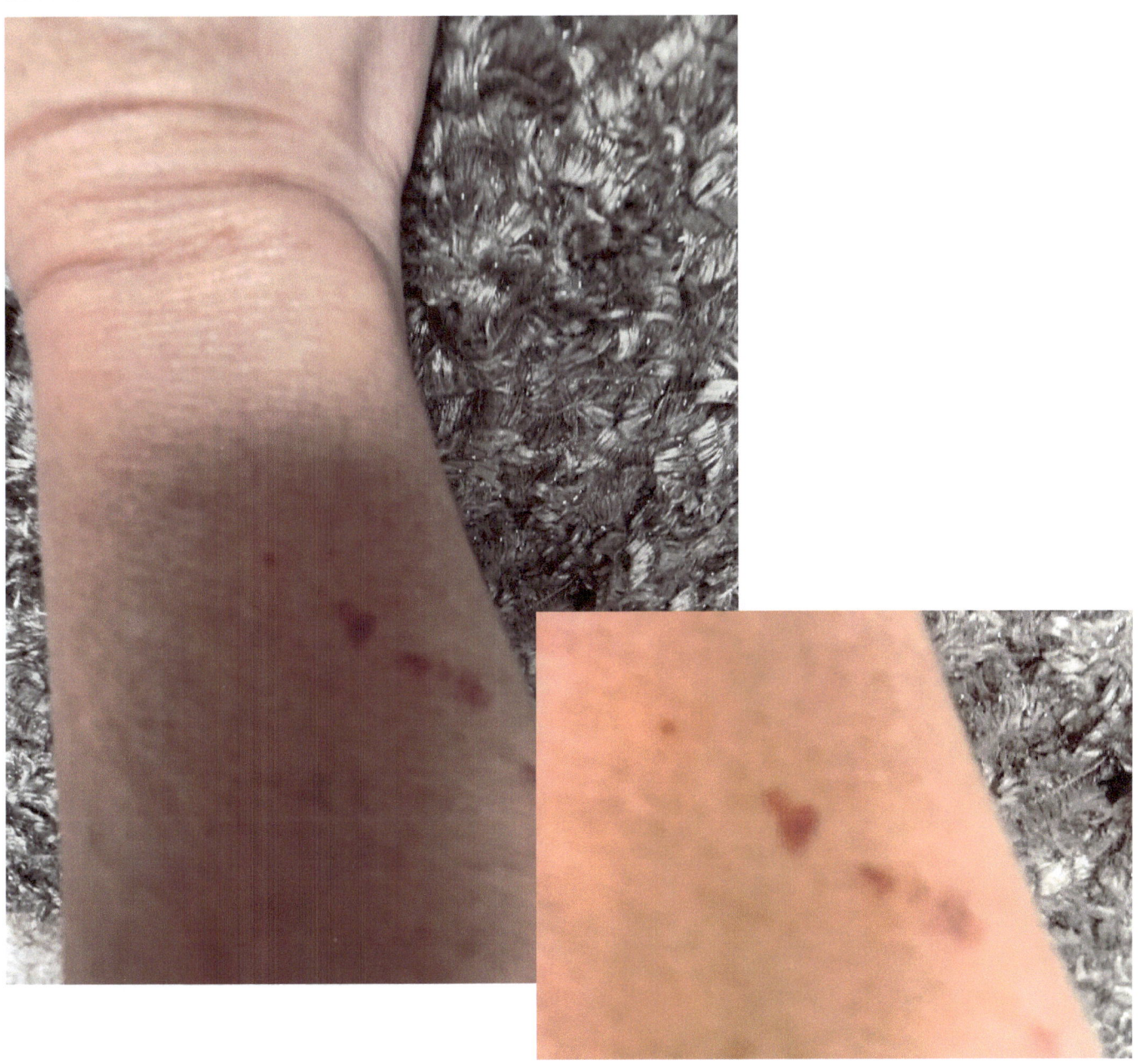

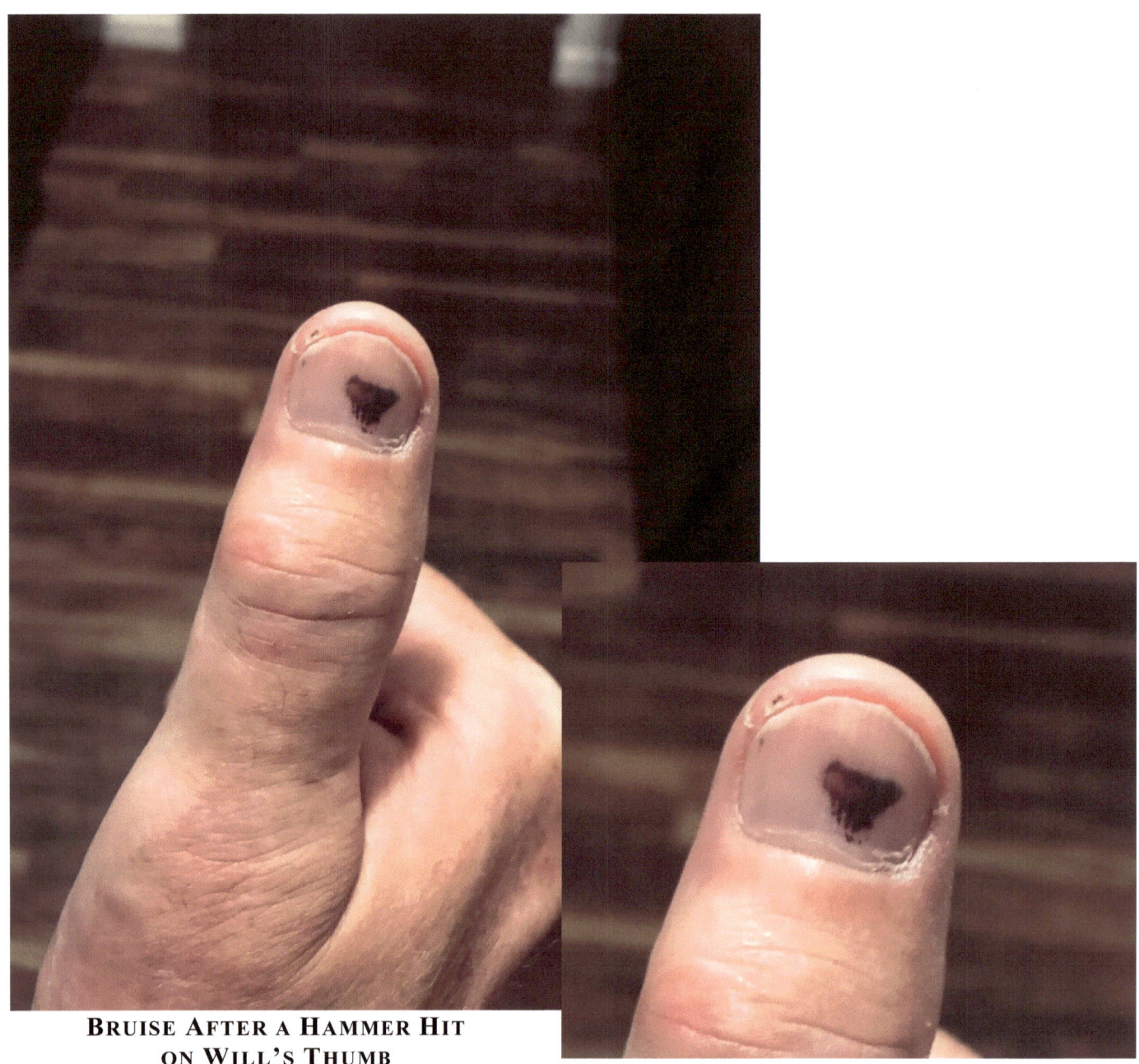

BRUISE AFTER A HAMMER HIT ON WILL'S THUMB

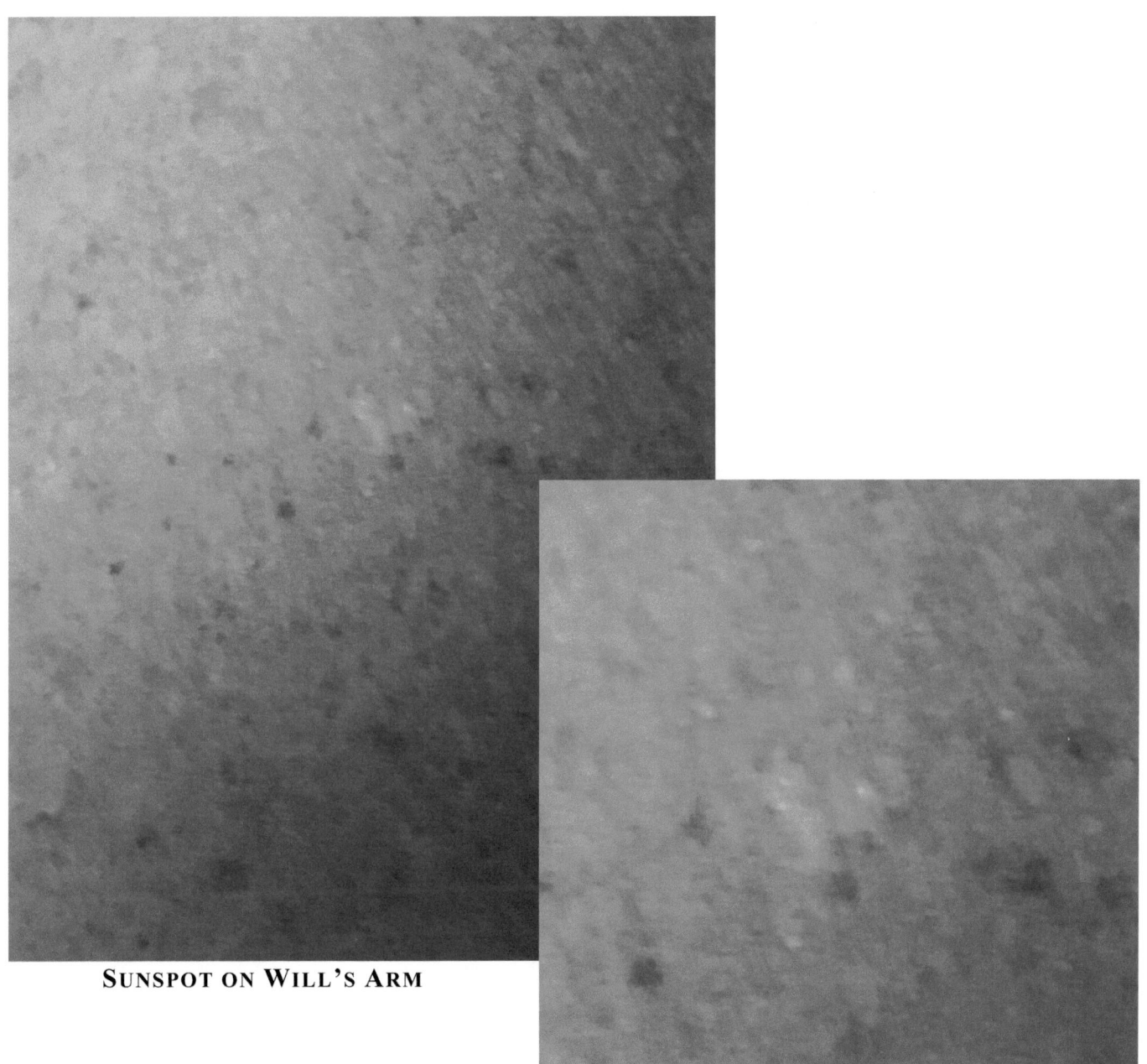

SUNSPOT ON WILL'S ARM

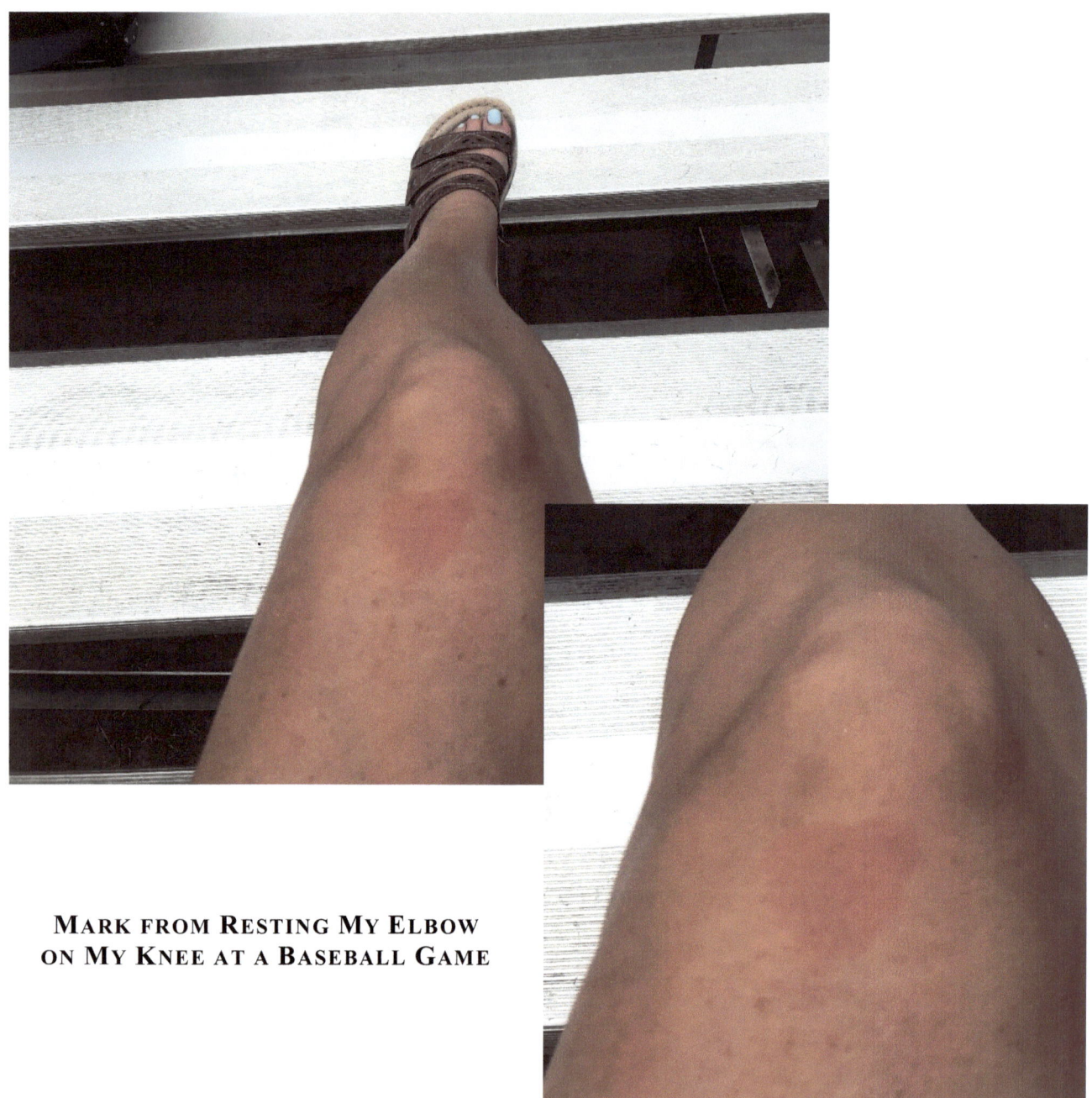

MARK FROM RESTING MY ELBOW ON MY KNEE AT A BASEBALL GAME

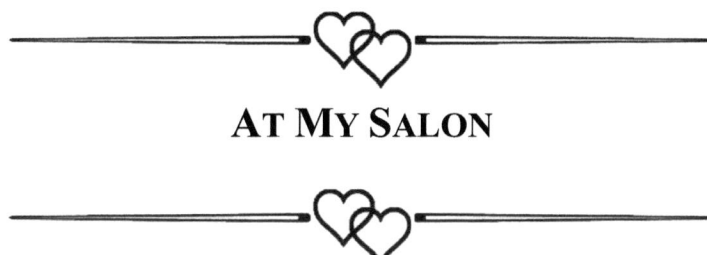

AT MY SALON

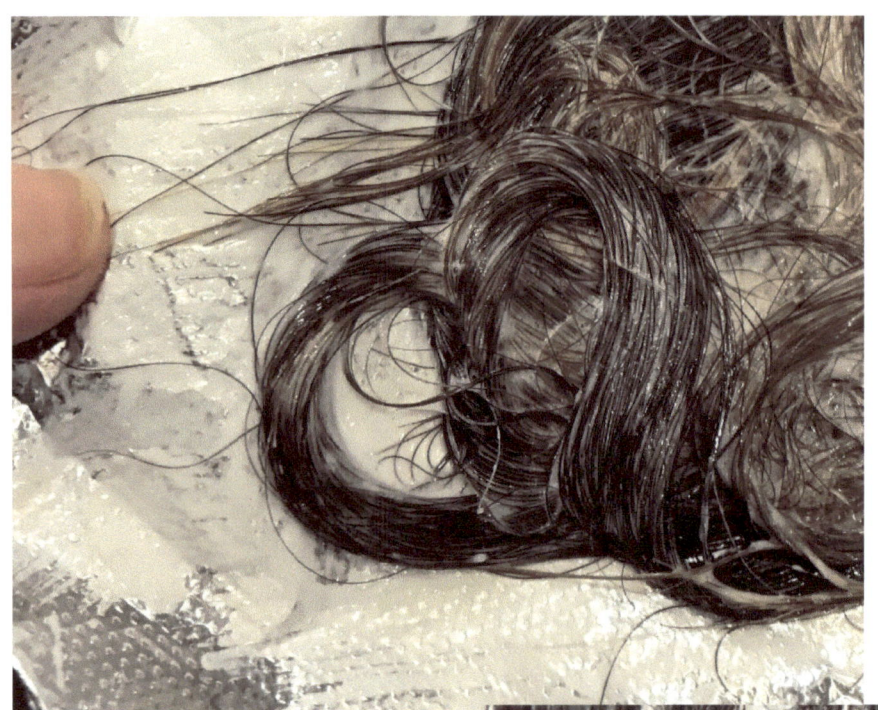

HAIR IN FOIL

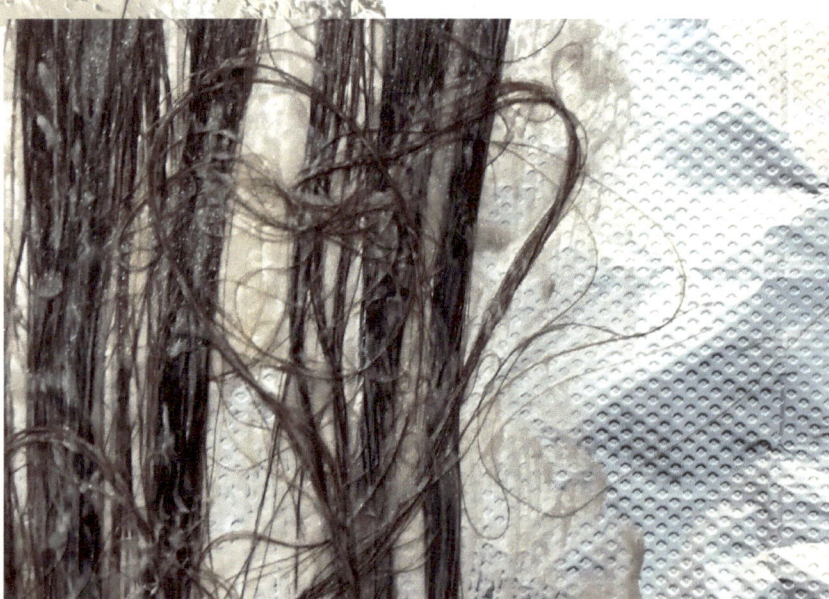

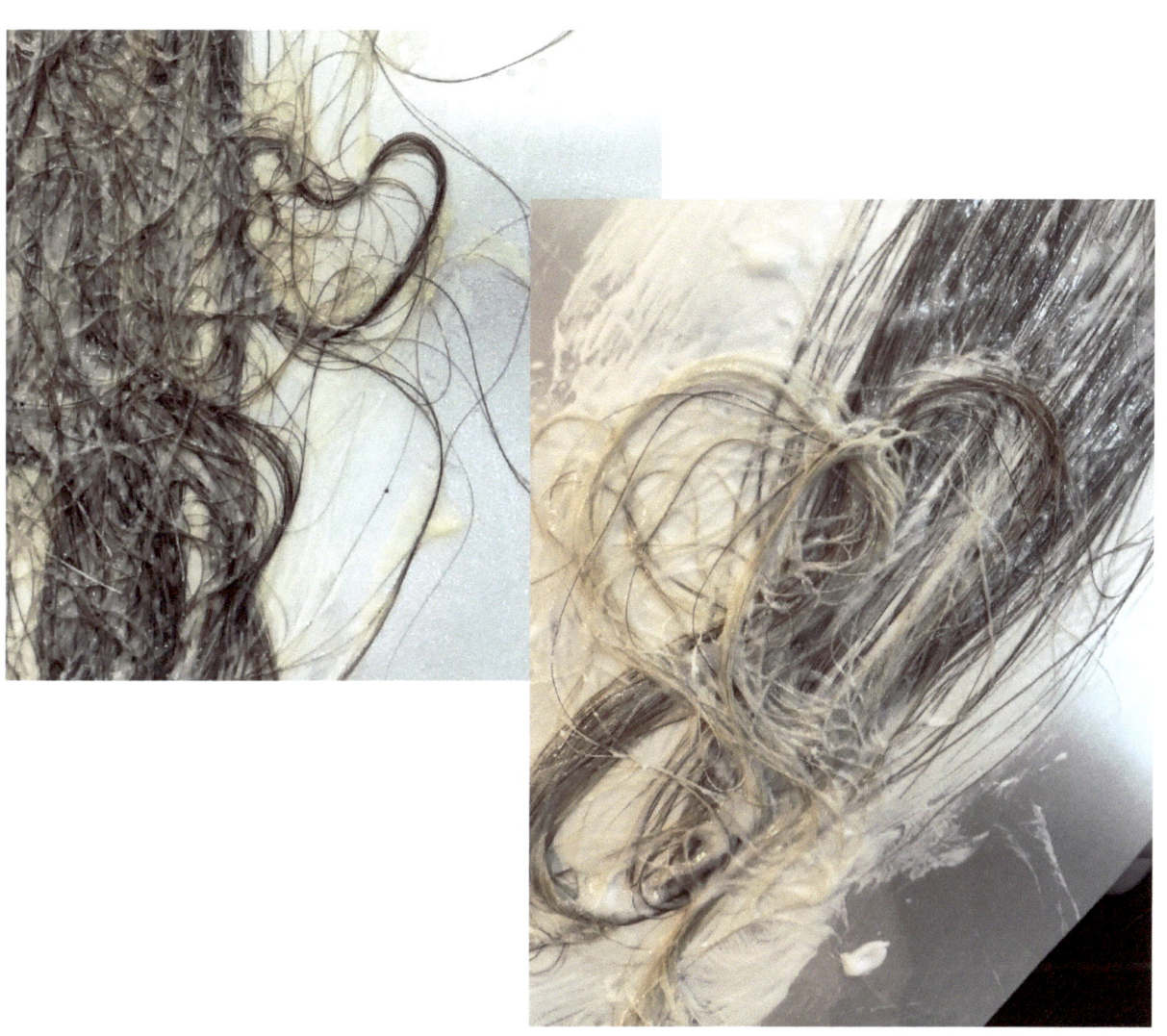

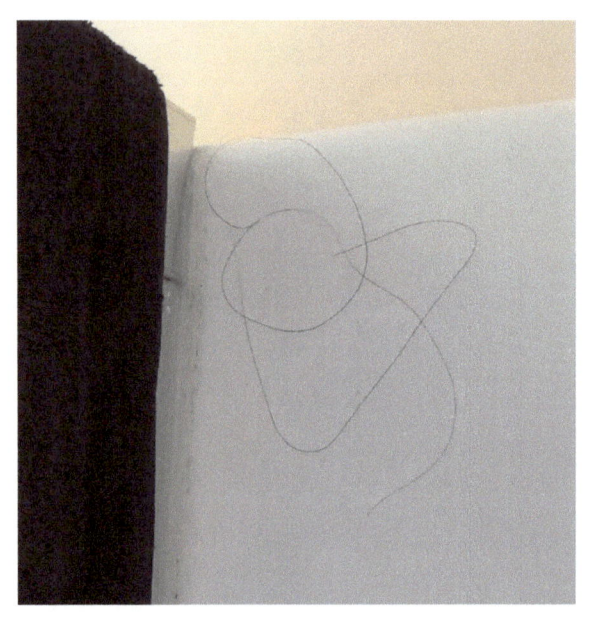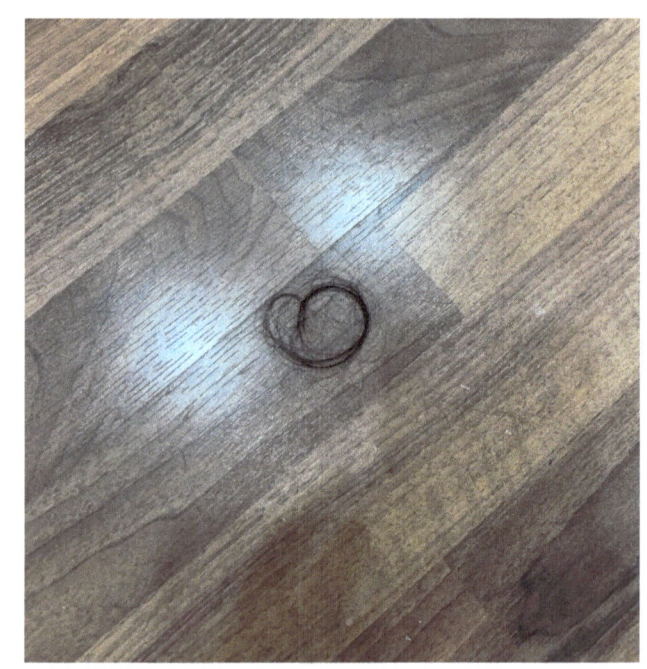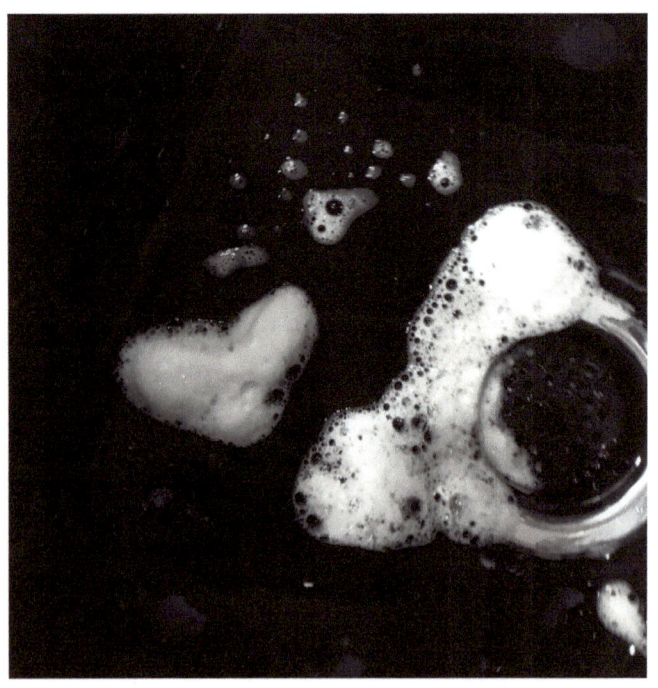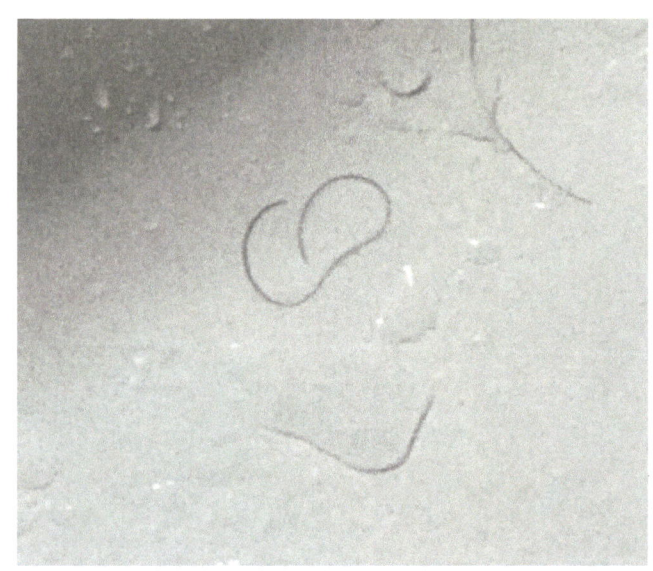

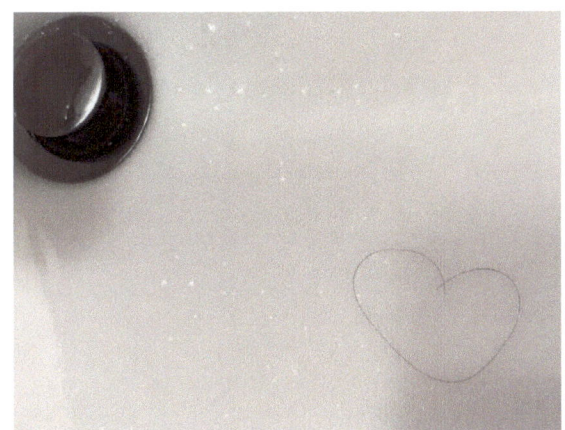

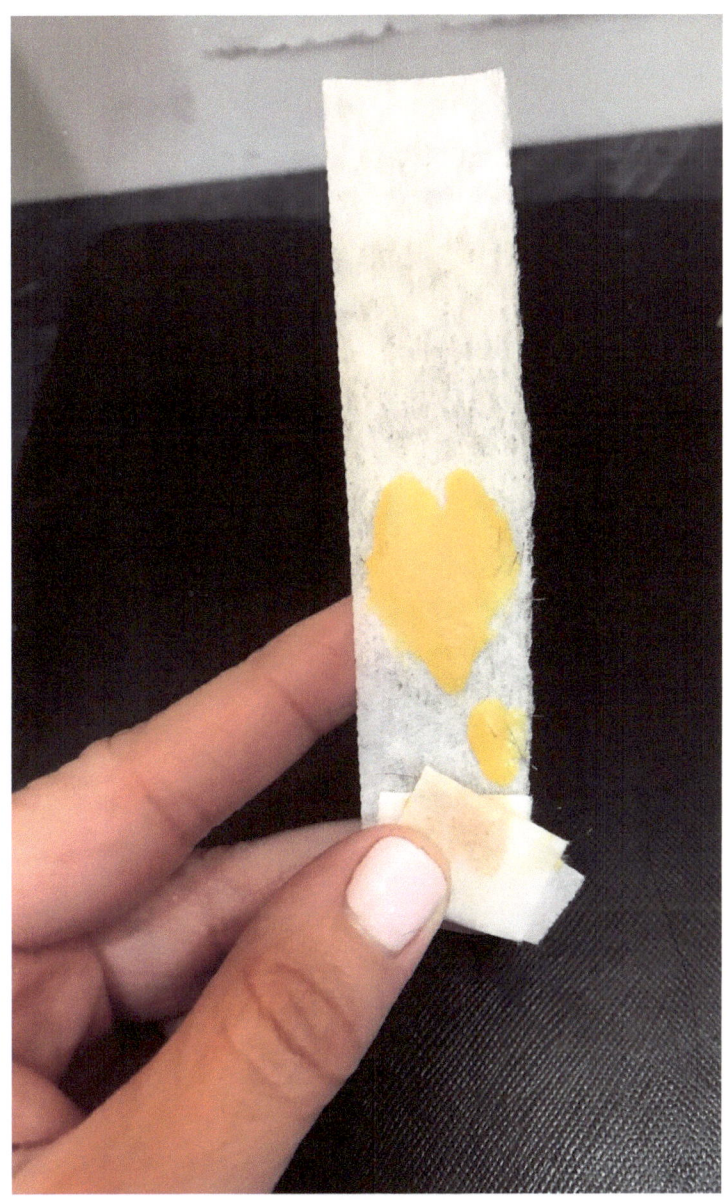

EYEBROW WAX STRIP

About the Author

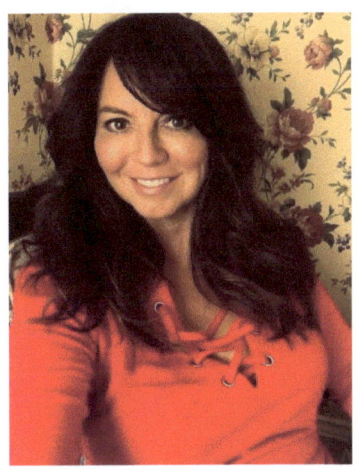

Kim Timmerman is a salon owner/hair stylist, mom and lives in the suburbs of St Louis, MO. For ten years, she has been an advocate for heart health awareness for women, which is the number one killer of women. It reigns above all cancers combined. One in three women die from heart disease and most are unaware of this fact. To put it into perspective 1 in 30 die from breast cancer.

Kim accumulated so many pictures she toyed with the idea to make a calendar. She wanted to donate partial profits from the calendar to *Go Red for Women*. After telling her boyfriend Will her plan, he suggested she publish a book of all her great photos for the fundraiser instead of a calendar. She took him up on his advice and now *Hearts in Abundance* has come to fruition.

Kim wants to share her journey and inspire us to slow down and open our eyes to all the love and beauty in everyday things all around us. And please take care of your heart and the hearts of those you love. Familiarize yourself with the signs and symptoms of heart attacks in women.

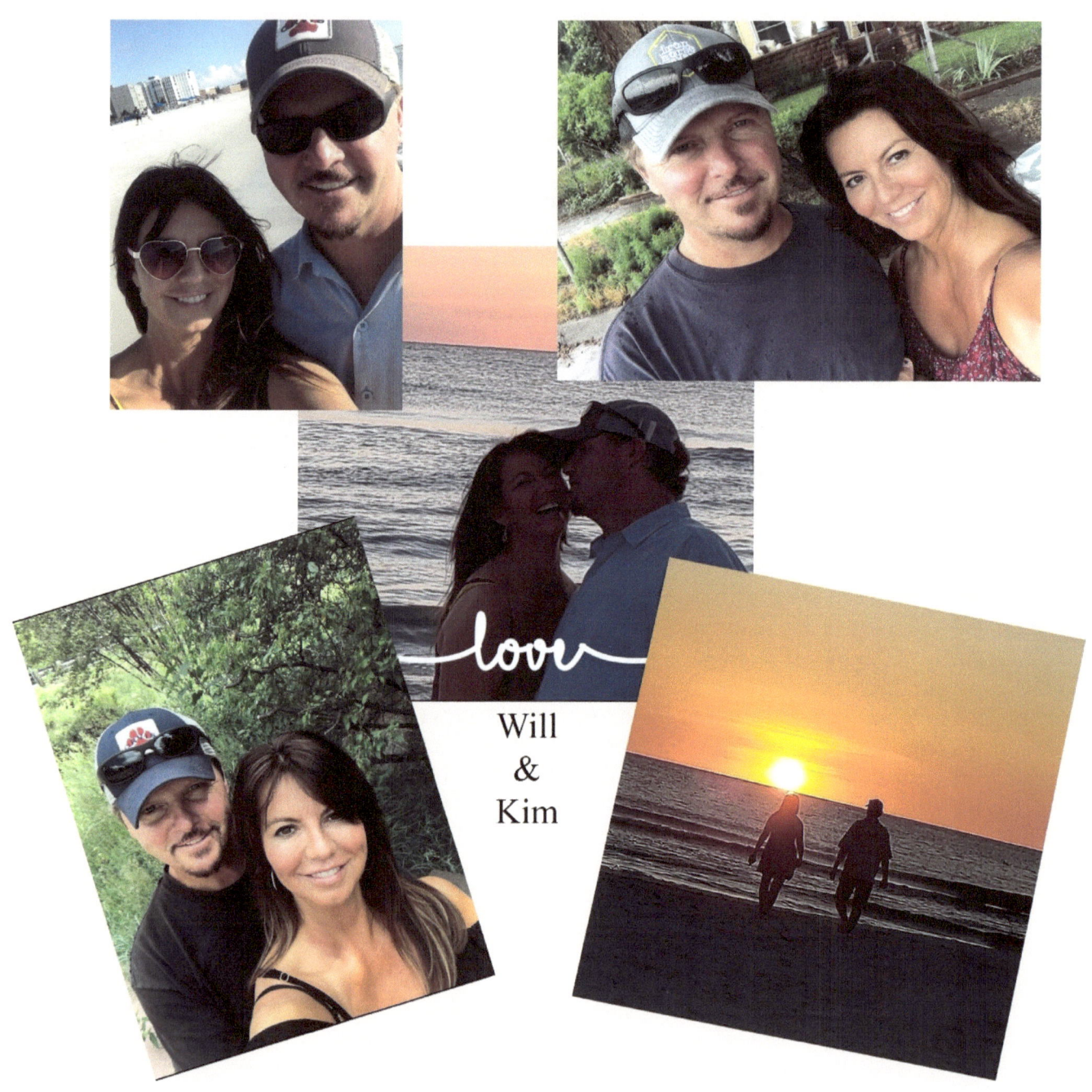

Will
&
Kim

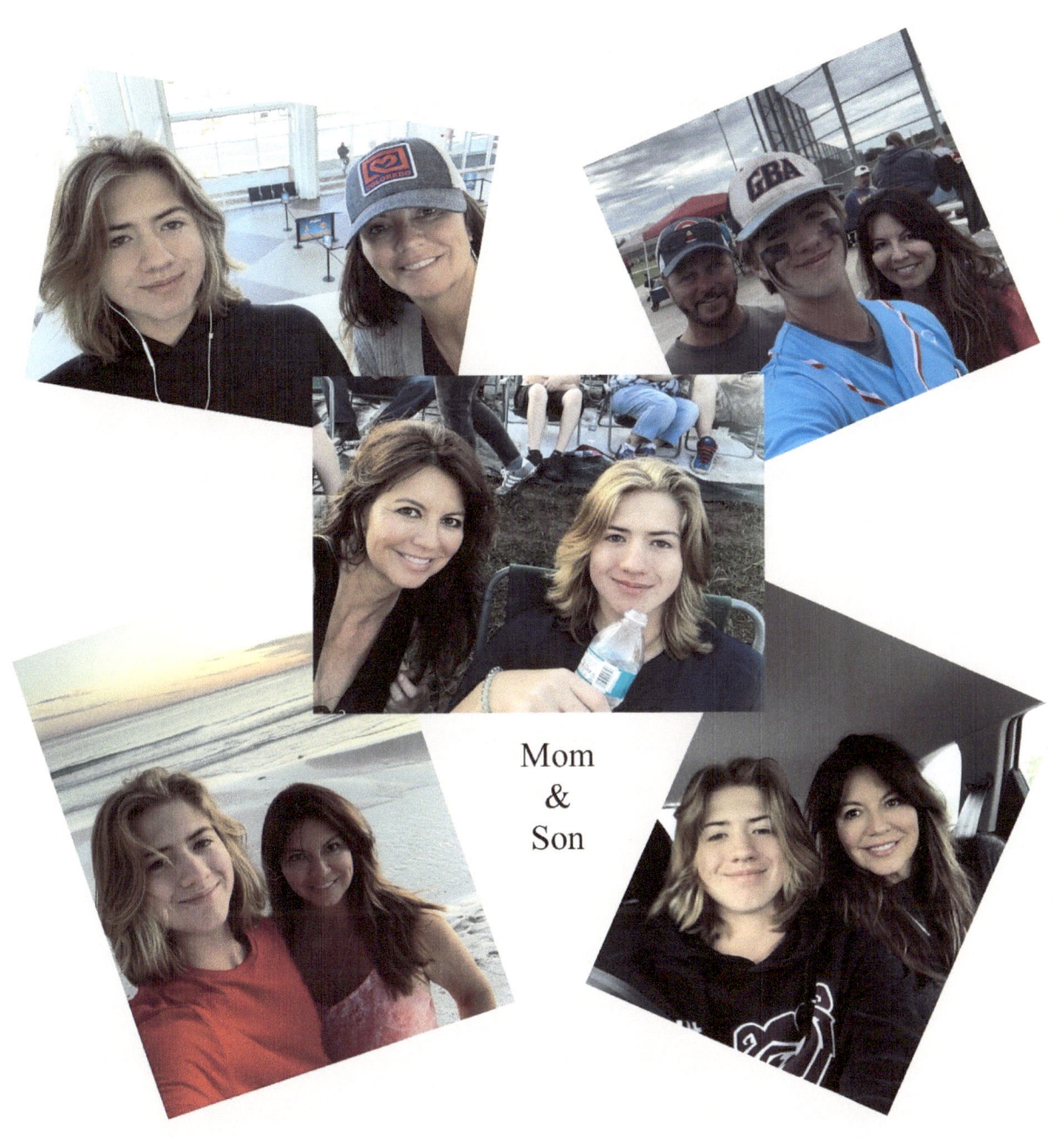

Mom & Son

www.ingramcontent.com/pod-product-compliance
Lightning Source LLC
Chambersburg PA
CBHW051155220526
45473CB00003B/780